RAND

Countywide Evaluation of the Long-Term Family Self-Sufficiency Plan

Establishing the Baselines

Robert F. Schoeni, Jeanne Ringel, John Hedderson, Paul S. Steinberg, Laura Hickman, Eric Eide, Marian Bussey, John Fluke, Jacob Alex Klerman

Prepared for
County of Los Angeles

RAND Labor & Population

The research described in this report was conducted by RAND Labor & Population for the County of Los Angeles.

Library of Congress Cataloging-in-Publication Data

Countywide evaluation of the long-term family self-sufficiency plan: establishing the baselines
   Robert F. Schoeni ... [et al.].
      p. cm.
   T.p. has countrywide but data sheet and prefatory matter indicate that it should be countywide.
   "MR-1466."
   Includes bibliographical references.
   ISBN 0-8330-3172-4
   1. Welfare recipients—Employment—California—Los Angeles County. 2. Public welfare—California—Los Angeles County. 3. California Work Opportunity and Responsibility to Kids (Program) I. Title: LTFSS plan countywide evaluation. II. Schoeni, Robert F.

HV98.C2 L795 2002
362.5'8'09794—dc21

                                                                    2002021365

RAND is a nonprofit institution that helps improve policy and decisionmaking through research and analysis. RAND® is a registered trademark. RAND's publications do not necessarily reflect the opinions or policies of its research sponsors.

Published 2002 by RAND
1700 Main Street, P.O. Box 2138, Santa Monica, CA 90407-2138
1200 South Hayes Street, Arlington, VA 22202-5050
201 North Craig Street, Suite 202, Pittsburgh, PA 15213
RAND URL: http://www.rand.org/
To order RAND documents or to obtain additional information, contact Distribution Services: Telephone: (310) 451-7002; Fax: (310) 451-6915; Email: order@rand.org

PREFACE

The Los Angeles County Board of Supervisors (Board) adopted the Long-Term Family Self-Sufficiency (LTFSS) Plan on November 16, 1999. The LTFSS Plan consists of 46 projects whose goal is to promote self-sufficiency among families that are participating in the California Work Opportunity and Responsibility to Kids (CalWORKs) program, among former CalWORKs families, and among other low-income families. The Chief Administrative Office (CAO) is the lead agency responsible for implementing the evaluation of the LTFSS Plan. On December 5, 2000, the Board approved the implementation plan for the evaluation of the LTFSS Plan, Project #46. Following an open and competitive bidding process, the Board awarded RAND a contract to conduct a Countywide evaluation of the LTFSS Plan, and a subcontract was awarded to Walter R. McDonald and Associates (WRMA) to work jointly with RAND on the evaluation. Elaine Reardon is the project director, and John Hedderson is WRMA's project leader. Marian Bussey and John Fluke, who are authors on this report, are members of the WRMA team.

To evaluate the performance of the 46 projects, the County selected 26 indicators, including five "headline indicators." One objective of the evaluation is to determine the baseline performance of the County on the 26 indicators, and, in particular, on the five headline indicators. This RAND report provides the baseline trends for the five headline indicators and describes the factors that have caused the trends to appear as they do—i.e., tells the "story behind the baseline." The analysis presented in this report represents work completed as of the end of August 2001. Some of the analyses have been updated with data released through late 2001. Even the latest released data do not cover the period following the tragedy of September 2001. Therefore, the forecasts also do not adjust for the effects of those events or the recession that followed.

For more information about RAND's evaluation of the LTFSS Plan, contact:

Elaine Reardon
Project Director and Associate Economist
RAND
1700 Main Street
Santa Monica, CA 90407

CONTENTS

TABLES

- ix -

FIGURES

EXECUTIVE SUMMARY

INTRODUCTION

Responding to new opportunities and new funding, the Los Angeles County Board of Supervisors (Board) adopted a Long-Term Family Self-Sufficiency (LTFSS) Plan on November 16, 1999. The Plan envisions 46 interrelated projects with the common goal of promoting sustained self-sufficiency for California Work Opportunity and Responsibility to Kids (CalWORKs) families, for former CalWORKs families, and for other low-income families in Los Angeles County.

Implementation of the Plan is proceeding under a results-based accountability framework. On June 14, 1999, the County Board approved the outcomes and indicators to measure the progress of the 46 projects in the Plan in achieving the intended result of self-sufficiency. As part of this framework, the County selected five outcome areas of population well-being, 26 indicators within those outcome areas to measure the progress of the 46 projects in meeting the outcomes, and five "headline indicators"—one from within each outcome area—from among the 26 indicators. The five "headline indicators"—low birth weight births, domestic violence arrests, annual income under poverty level, personal behaviors harmful to self or others, and teenage high school graduation—are being used to track each of the five outcome areas—Good Health; Safety and survival; Economic Well-Being; Social and Emotional Well-Being; and Education/Workforce Readiness, respectively. Each headline indicator is meant to serve as a proxy for the broader set of indicators within each outcome area. Schoeni and Hedderson (2001) provide a more detailed discussion of these headline indicators and of the broader set of indicators, as well as detailed descriptions of the databases to be used in estimating indicators.

This report presents estimates of the indicators for the County; lays out a "baseline" trend for the indicators; describes the factors that have caused the baseline trends for the headline indicators to appear as they do, i.e., tells the "story behind the baseline"; and provides forecasts for the five headline indicators.

GOOD HEALTH: LOW BIRTH WEIGHT BIRTHS

As shown in Figure E.1, the percentage of infants born weighing less than 2,500 grams—the low birth weight rate—has been increasing in the County during the 1990s. The increase in the percentage of low weight births is not unique to Los Angeles County; it has been observed for the rest of California and the nation as well. The increase of the 1990s represents a departure from improvements in low birth weight rates that were made nationally during the 1960s and 1970s. Increases in the percentage of infants born with low birth weight are of concern because such infants face an elevated risk of a wide variety of health and developmental problems or conditions. In addition, low birth weight significantly increases the risk of infant mortality (Hack et al., 1995; Paneth, 1995).

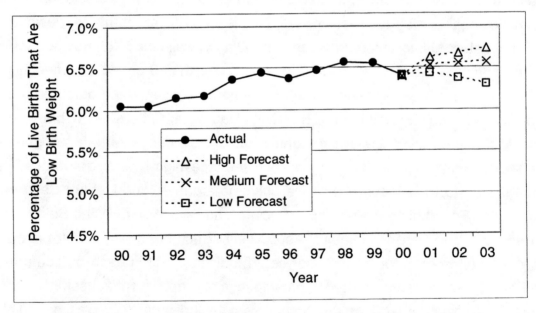

Figure E.1—Low Birth Weight Births in Los Angeles County: 1990–2000 and Forecasts

- The increase in low birth weight births during the 1990s can be attributed primarily to increases in the percentage of multiple births. Twins, triplets, and higher-order births tend to be born at much lower weights than singletons. The percentage of multiple births increased 25 percent during this time period.

- The low birth weight birth rate among single births has remained relatively constant over the same time period.

- Although estimates of the low birth weight birth rate are not available for CalWORKs participants, it is expected that the low birth weight birth rate did not increase during the 1990s for lower-income women, such as those on CalWORKs. This conclusion is based on the fact that the increase in multiple births was largely the result of an increase in the use of fertility treatments, which are mostly used by higher-income women. Future analysis will attempt to directly examine low birth weight births among CalWORKs participants.

- The prevalence of maternal behaviors associated with low birth weight, such as smoking or drinking during pregnancy, has declined nationally. There are no data available to determine whether this healthy trend differs in Los Angeles County.

- Shifts in the racial/ethnic composition of the population in the County do not explain the increases in the rate of low birth weight births in the 1990s.

- The mid-level forecasts imply that, in the absence of the LTFSS Plan, the share of births that are low birth weight will be 6.4 percent by 2003, which is similar to the most recent estimates from 2000. The low and high estimates imply low birth weight rates of 6.3 percent and 6.7 percent, respectively.

SAFETY AND SURVIVAL: DOMESTIC VIOLENCE ARRESTS

Arrests for domestic violence have been increasing in the County over the last decade, as shown in Figure E.2. Between 1988 and 1998, the total number of arrests per year increased 38 percent, from 12,435 to 17,190. Because population grew as well, the domestic violence arrest rate—measured as the number of arrests per 100,000 of the population age 18 and over—grew at a slightly slower rate, from 197.6 to 276.7 between 1988 and 1997, declining thereafter such that by 2000, it was 211.7 (Figure E.2). This trend toward more arrests and then a sharp decline has also been observed for the rest of the state.

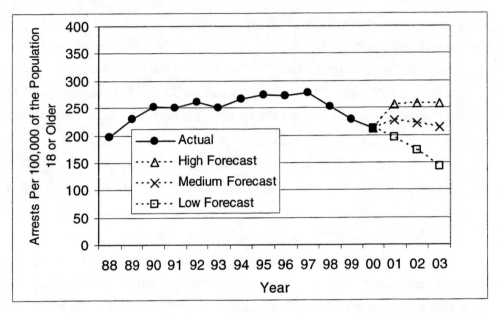

Figure E.2—Domestic Violence Arrest Rate in Los Angeles County: 1988–2000 and Forecasts

- Arrest rates for domestic violence reflect three distinct components: (1) the number of domestic violence incidents, (2) the willingness of victims and witnesses to report an incident, and (3) police behavior once police receive a report of an incident.

- The increases in the domestic violence arrest rate through 1997 can be viewed as an improvement because they appear to be driven by positive changes in police behavior. The cause of the decline since 1997 is unclear, although some nationwide evidence suggests that domestic violence and, therefore, perhaps arrests, are declining.

- During this time period, California initiated a number of changes specifically targeted toward increasing police use of arrest in domestic violence situations. In addition to legislative efforts, many local organizations have been established to address domestic violence, including improving police response.

- According to data from the National Crime Victimization Survey (NCVS), domestic violence toward females has been on the decline since 1993 (Greenfeld et al., 1998; Rennison, 2001). While we do not have data specific to California, this national trend suggests that domestic violence incidents may have also been in decline in Los Angeles County.

- The forecasts imply that by 2003 the domestic violence arrest rate will most likely fall in the range of 143 to 258 arrests per 100,000 of the population age 18 and over.

ECONOMIC WELL-BEING: ANNUAL INCOME UNDER POVERTY LEVEL

As shown in Figure E.3, the poverty rate—defined as the percentage of people living in families whose income is below the federal poverty threshold—has been declining rapidly since the mid-1990s. Almost 25 percent of Angelenos lived in poverty in 1994, but in the latest year for which data are available, 2000, 17 percent lived in poverty. Despite the substantial improvements since 1994, the long-run trend over the entire 25-year period for which data are available has been toward higher poverty.

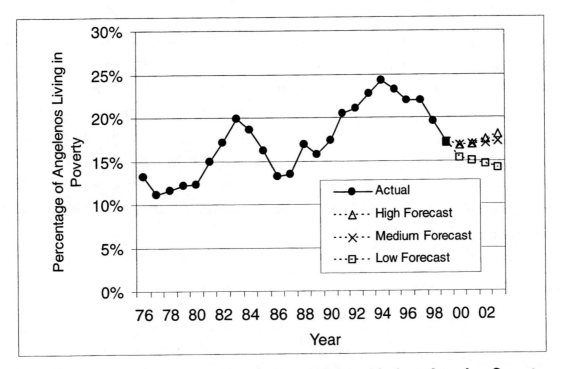

Figure E.3—Annual Income under Poverty Level in Los Angeles County: 1976–2000 and Forecasts

- The short-run fluctuations in poverty result primarily from changes in the macroeconomy. In addition, some of the recent decline is likely associated with changes in welfare policy.
- The long-run increase in poverty can be viewed in terms of the racial/ethnic composition of the population. Compared to 25 years ago, a higher percentage of Angelenos today are Hispanic, a racial/ethnic group with a high poverty rate.
- Although the latest data are for 2000, it is expected that poverty continued to fall in 2001, given that the economy in Los Angeles expanded during the past year. Poverty in the next few years will be heavily influenced by the economy, ongoing demographic changes, and welfare and poverty policy.
- The forecasts depend heavily on future economic conditions, which are difficult to predict. By 2003, the forecasts of poverty range from a low of 14 percent to a high of 18 percent.

SOCIAL AND EMOTIONAL WELL-BEING: PERSONAL BEHAVIOR HARMFUL TO SELF OR OTHERS

Personal behavior harmful to self or others is measured with child abuse and neglect, which, in turn, is defined as the number of substantiated child abuse and neglect cases per 1,000 children in the population. Figure E.4 shows that child abuse and neglect declined in the County during the 1990s, but the decline was not monotonic. Between 1990 and 1992, the rate fell from 32 to 23 cases per 1,000. However, this fall was followed by a substantial rise to 37 cases by 1996. After 1996, the rate declined in each of the subsequent four years, leaving the rate at 15 cases per 1,000, or one-half the level that existed at the beginning of the decade.

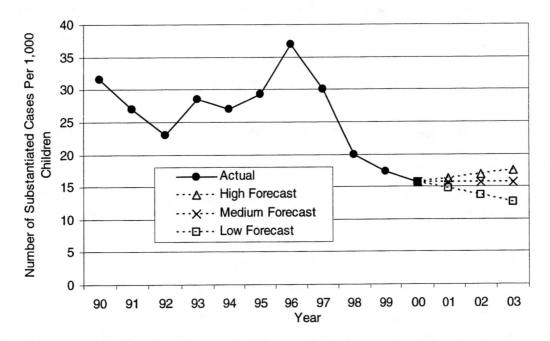

Figure E.4—Child Abuse and Neglect per 1,000 Children in Los Angeles County: 1990–2000 and Forecasts

- The change in the rate of substantiated cases of child abuse and neglect may be attributed to changes in reporting, a change in the response of child safety officials, and/or actual changes in the incidence of child abuse. Each of these factors is affected by public awareness of preventive efforts and community and environmental trends.

- It is not yet known for certain which aspects are reflected in the changes observed in the 1990s.

- The recession of the early to mid-1990s, which caused an increase in poverty and a rise in welfare participation, was most likely an important cause of the increase in the child abuse and neglect rate; the recession had this impact by affecting parental stress and, in turn, child safety. Similarly, the subsequent improvements in the labor market and poverty likely contributed to the decline in the late 1990s.

- At the beginning of the 1990s, the rate of substantiated child abuse and neglect was two and one-half times higher in the County than in the rest of the nation. This gap declined substantially in subsequent years, with rates being 41 percent higher in Los Angeles County than in the rest of the nation in 1999.

- The "medium" forecasts imply that child abuse and neglect will hold steady near its 2000 rate of 15.7 cases per 1,000. The low and high forecasts for 2003 range from 12.6 to 17.5 cases per 1,000.

EDUCATIONAL AND WORKFORCE READINESS: TEENAGE HIGH SCHOOL GRADUATION

We measure education and workforce readiness with the teenage high school graduation rate, which is defined as the ratio of the number of public high school graduates in a given year divided by the number of ninth-graders in public schools three academic years earlier and which is expressed as a percentage. As Figure E.5 shows, the high school graduation rate was virtually unchanged in Los Angeles County during the period for which estimates are available, 1997–2000. The estimates imply that 62 percent of ninth-graders graduate from high school within four years.

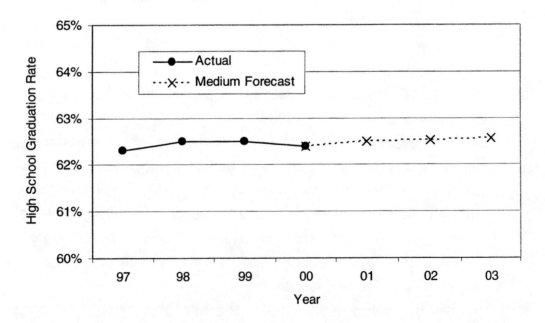

Figure E.5—High School Graduation Rate in Los Angeles County: 1997–2000 and Forecasts

- This rate is lower than the rate in the rest of California, where 71 percent of ninth-graders in 1997 graduated in 2000. Although the graduation rate is higher in California, it follows a similar flat trend, as it does in the United States.
- Research suggests that the factors affecting high school completion include race/ethnicity, family background, labor market forces, and public policy.
- This indicator draws on the best available data; however, the measure suffers from notable limitations. Most important, the measure assumes there is no movement of students in or out of the County during the high school years, or that at least the movements in and out are perfectly offsetting. Alternative measures should be investigated.
- Teen high school graduation has held steady during recent years, and there is no reason to expect that it would have changed substantially (by even half a percentage point) in the coming years in the absence of LTFSS Plan. We therefore present only a single forecast.

NEXT STEPS

This report provides the County with the baseline trends. The ultimate goal—but not the subject of this document—is to update the trendlines for the indicators as the LTFSS Plan is implemented and then compare these trendlines for the period before and after the LTFSS Plan has been implemented to determine net impacts. The updating will occur in each year of the three-year contract between RAND and the County. Baseline outcome data will be compared to post-Plan outcomes when those data become available. The LTFSS Plan will most likely be fully implemented by the end of 2002, which suggests that data are needed for at least 2002 and 2003 before post-Plan outcomes can be measured. In addition, delays in the release of data sources range from six months to two years, implying that estimates for 2002 and 2003 will be available no sooner than 2004 and, in many cases, not until 2005.

In the meantime, the measurement of the indicators will proceed along three dimensions. First, as more-recent data become available in the future, these data will be analyzed and the indicators measured, with the estimates added to the current charts. Second, measurement of the indicators for additional subgroups will be explored. Third, the items on the Data Development Agenda will be addressed.

ACKNOWLEDGMENTS

We thank Amy Cox, Jacob Klerman, Elaine Reardon, and the Chief Administrative Office (CAO), Service Integration Branch (SIB) of Los Angeles County for comments, and Christopher Dirks, David Kurth, Christina Pitcher, and Benson Wong for assistance in preparing the report.

ACRONYMS

AFDC	Aid to Families with Dependent Children
AHS	American Housing Survey
Board	Board of Supervisors
BRFSS	Behavioral Risk Factor Surveillance System
CalWORKs	California Work Opportunity and Responsibility to Kids Act of 1997
CAO	Chief Administrative Office
CDE	California Department of Education
CDF	California Department of Finance
CDJ	California Department of Justice
CDSS	California Department of Social Services
CPC	Children's Planning Council
CPS	Current Population Survey
CTNA	CalWORKs Transportation Needs Assessment Survey
DCFS	Department of Children and Family Services
DPSS	Department of Public Social Services
EDD	Employment Development Department
EITC	Earned Income Tax Credit
GAIN	Greater Avenues for Independence
GED	General Education Degree
HSAA	High School attendance area
JTPA	Job Training Partnership Act
LACHS	Los Angeles County Health Survey
LAC DAO	Los Angeles County District Attorney's Office
LAC DCFS	Los Angeles County Department of Children and Family Services
LAC DHS	Los Angeles County Department of Health Services
LAC PROB	Los Angeles County Probation Department
LTFSS	Long-Term Family Self-Sufficiency
MEDS	Medi-Cal Eligibility Determination System
NCES	National Center for Education Statistics
NCVS	National Crime Victimization Survey

NDTF	New Directions Task Force
ORG	Outgoing Rotation Group
SD	Supervisorial District
SPA	Service Planning Area
SSI	Supplemental Security Income
TANF	Temporary Assistance for Needy Families
WIC	Women, Infants, and Children program
WRMA	Walter R. McDonald and Associates

1. INTRODUCTION

BACKGROUND

As part of welfare reform, Los Angeles County conducted a broad-based effort to review the delivery of services to families enrolled in the California Work Opportunity and Responsibility to Kids (CalWORKs) program, to former CalWORKs families, and to other low-income families by County health and human service agencies. This effort of the County's New Directions Task Force (NDTF) resulted in a report that serves as the basis for the Long-Term Family Self-Sufficiency (LTFSS) Plan, which was adopted by the County's Board of Supervisors (Board) on November 16, 1999 (New Directions Task Force, 1999). The LTFSS Plan consists of eight strategies to promote long-term family self-sufficiency:

1. Promoting self-sustaining employment
2. Ensuring access to health care
3. Supporting stable housing
4. Helping teens become self-sufficient adults
5. Promoting youth literacy
6. Curbing violence
7. Building strong families
8. Integrating the human services delivery system.

Implementation of the Plan is proceeding under a results-based accountability framework (Friedman, 2001). Crucial to that framework is a set of desired *outcomes*. Following the County's Strategic Plan for Children, Youth, and Families as proposed by the County's Children's Planning Council (CPC) (Los Angeles County Children's Planning Council, 1998) and as adopted by the Board on January 26, 1993, the LTFSS Plan specifies five desired outcomes that the 46 projects should contribute to achieving:

1. Good health
2. Safety and survival
3. Economic well-being
4. Social and emotional well-being
5. Educational and workforce readiness.

Also crucial to the framework is a set of indicators against which the five outcomes are to be measured. More specifically, the LTFSS Plan identified 26 *indicators* to use in evaluating progress toward achieving the eight strategies and five outcomes.

OBJECTIVE

As part of an ongoing contract with the Los Angeles County Chief Administrative Office (CAO), RAND is conducting the Countywide Evaluation of the LTFSS Plan. This report is one in a series of reports that will be prepared as part of the evaluation. An earlier report evaluated the data sources that can be used to measure the 26 indicators. In particular, for each of the 26 indicators, the report precisely defined the indicator; determined the data sets that could be used for estimation; determined the availability of the estimates by time period, CalWORKs status, income, race/ethnicity, language, and geography; and assessed the quality of the estimates that could be obtained. In addition, the report identified five "headline indicators" from the original 26 that will be used to track each of the five outcome areas and placed nine of the original 26 indicators on the Countywide Evaluation's Data Development Agenda because data for these indicators are either sparse or nonexistent (Hedderson and Schoeni, 2001).

This report presents estimates of the indicators for Los Angeles County; lays out a "baseline" trend for the headline indicators; describes the factors that have caused the baseline trends to appear as they do for each of the headline indicators, i.e., tells the "story behind the baseline"; and provides forecasts for the five headline indicators. The ultimate goal—but not the subject of this document—is to update the trendlines for the indicators as the LTFSS Plan is implemented and then compare these trendlines for the period before and after the LTFSS Plan has been implemented to determine net impacts. The updating will occur in each year of the three-year contract between RAND and the County. Baseline outcome data will be compared to post-Plan outcomes when those data become available. The LTFSS Plan will most likely be fully implemented by the end of 2002, which suggests that data are needed for at least 2002 and 2003 before post-Plan outcomes can be measured. In addition, delays in the release of data sources range from six months to two years, implying that estimates for 2002 and 2003 will be available no sooner than 2004 and, in many cases, not until 2005.

ORGANIZATION OF THIS REPORT

The organization of this document corresponds to the five outcome areas, with one chapter devoted to each of the five areas: good health, safety and survival, economic well-being, social and emotional well-being, and education/workforce readiness. Each chapter begins with a section that establishes the baseline trend in the headline indicator using the most recent data. In particular, a figure is shown that displays the Countywide trend and, when data are available, shows recent changes in relationship to historical patterns.

The second section in each chapter presents the story behind the baseline trend—the reasons or factors why the trend appears as it does. The "story" is developed using information from a variety of sources. First, we consulted with experts and examined evidence from the research literature on the factors believed to influence the headline indicator. Second, we determined the extent to which these factors have changed in the County to explain a change in the headline indicator. For example, the literature has shown that poverty is much higher for certain racial/ethnic groups; therefore, we estimate the extent to which the racial/ethnic composition of the population in Los Angeles County has changed in recent years. We then translate the changes in the factor—e.g., racial/ethnic composition—into the implied impact on the headline indicator—e.g., poverty—based on the relationships estimated in the research literature.

The third section briefly describes each of the 46 LTFSS Plan projects that are expected to affect the given headline indicator.

The fourth section presents forecasts of the headline indicators through 2003 *assuming that the LTFSS Plan would not have been implemented.* The forecasts are added to the original figure that displays the baseline trend; in the text, we discuss the direction in which the County is likely to be headed over that time frame. As with all forecasts, they are highly uncertain. In all cases, we provide a set of three forecasts that represent the range of possibilities. The methods and factors influencing the forecasts, which are discussed within each of the five outcomes chapters, differ across headline indicators.

The fifth section in each chapter briefly examines the trends in the other, non-headline indicators within the outcome area. In some cases, these trends inform the interpretation of the changes in the headline indicators.

The final section in each chapter provides a summary of the key conclusions in the chapter.

Following Chapters 2–6 on the five outcomes, a final chapter describes the next steps that will be taken to complete the Countywide Evaluation.

Appendix A lists the 46 projects that make up the LTFSS Plan, the headline indicators that each of these projects target, and the amount of initial funding that each project has been allocated. Appendix B reports the measurement for all 18 indicators in each year, including measurement for subgroups when they are available.[1] A variety of data sources is used to estimate the 18 indicators. To conserve space, the source for each estimate is not reported within Chapters 2–6. Instead, the data source for each indicator and its exact definition are reported in Appendix B.

---

[1]Of the original 26 indicators, nine have been placed on the Data Development Agenda, leaving 17 indicators for evaluation. However, an additional indicator—homicide rates—was added.

2. GOOD HEALTH: LOW BIRTH WEIGHT BIRTHS

Within the good health outcome area, the LTFSS Plan specified five indicators: (1) access to health care, (2) infant mortality, (3) low birth weight births, (4) births to teens, and (5) individuals without health insurance. Access to health care was placed on the Data Development Agenda. Low birth weight was chosen as the headline indicator because it is compelling, easily understood, and associated with other health outcomes. Moreover, the rate of low birth weight births can be accurately estimated for both the County as a whole and for several subgroups within the County. Therefore, the analysis focuses on the rate of low birth weight births, which is defined as the percentage of live births weighing less than 2,500 grams.

ESTABLISHING THE BASELINE

Figure 2.1 shows that the percentage of low birth weight births has been increasing in Los Angeles County during the 1990s. This upward trend is not unique to Los Angeles County; it has also been observed for the rest of California and the nation as well (data in Table B.2). The increases of the 1990s represent a departure from the improvements in low birth weight rates made nationally during the 1960s and 1970s (data not shown).[1] Increases in the percentage of infants born with low birth weight are of concern because such infants face an elevated risk of a wide variety of health and developmental problems or conditions. In addition, low birth weight significantly increases the risk of infant mortality (Hack et al., 1995; Paneth, 1995).

---

[1]We have received vital statistics data for California back to 1960; however, because of time constraints, we limited our analysis to the 1990s. As the project continues, we will analyze the data from the earlier periods and incorporate them into the baseline charts.

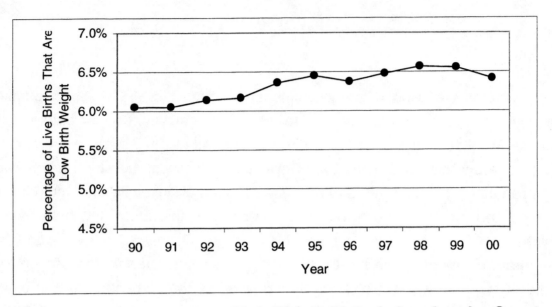

Figure 2.1—Percentage of Low Birth Weight Births in Los Angeles County: 1990–2000

THE STORY BEHIND THE BASELINE

In trying to understand the factors that might explain the increase in low birth weight births, we survey existing research in this area. To address the problem of low birth weight, researchers have focused on identifying the factors that cause infants to be born weighing less than 2,500 grams. This research suggests that maternal risk factors, such as smoking, drinking, and low maternal weight gain during pregnancy, are associated with higher rates of low birth weight. Demographic characteristics and characteristics of the birth have also been shown to affect low birth weight rates. The most important of these characteristics for explaining low birth weight are maternal race, gestational age at birth, and plurality of the birth. Changes in public policy can also have an effect on low birth weight rates by promoting healthy behaviors and/or providing greater access to medical services. Given the relationship between these factors and the probability of low birth weight, changes in these factors can help to explain the increases in the low birth weight rate that occurred during the 1990s. Each of these factors is discussed below.

Maternal Risk Factors

Smoking. Studies indicate that approximately 20 percent of the low birth weight rate can be attributed to maternal smoking during pregnancy. Specifically, smoking has been shown to decrease infant birth weight by approximately 200 grams (7 ounces) and to double the chance of a low birth weight delivery (U.S. Department of Health and Human Services, 1990). As such, an increase in the smoking rate among pregnant women in Los Angeles County during the 1990s could explain the increases in low birth weight observed in Figure 2.1.

However, available data suggest that smoking among pregnant women actually fell during this time period. Although there are no data available for the County specifically because California does not collect smoking information on the birth certificate, data from the rest of the United States indicate that maternal smoking fell by 35 percent between 1989 and 1999. (19.5 percent smoked in 1989 versus 12.6 percent in 1999.)

Drinking. Maternal drinking during pregnancy has also been shown to affect birth outcomes (Sampson et al., 1994; Roeleveld et al., 1992). Studies show that the risk of low birth weight increases twofold for women who consume 3–5 drinks per day during pregnancy as compared to women who do not drink (Mills et al., 1984). However, the effects of more moderate drinking during pregnancy are not as well established (Chomitz et al., 1995). Thus, if alcohol use during pregnancy has increased in the County during the 1990s, that could also help explain the increases shown in the figure.

However, at the national level, alcohol use during pregnancy has declined over the past several decades (Chomitz et al., 1995). Data from the Behavioral Risk Factor Surveillance System (BRFSS) show that nationally there was a reduction in maternal drinking during pregnancy from 23 percent in 1988 to 15 percent in 1995 (Ebrahim et al., 1998). There are no data available on maternal drinking during pregnancy for Los Angeles County, because the BRFSS does not sample enough people in the County to get reliable estimates. Further, California is one of only two states that does not report alcohol use on the birth certificate (Ventura et al., 2001). However, there is no reason to expect that the downward trend in maternal drinking has not occurred in Los Angeles County. If alcohol use during pregnancy in the County has followed the national trends, the overall reduction in drinking during the 1990s cannot explain the increase in low birth weight during the same time period.

Low Maternal Weight Gain. Low maternal weight gain during pregnancy is associated with increased rates of low birth weight births. In 1999, data for all states excluding California[2] show that the percentage of infants with low birth weight dropped steadily with increases in maternal weight gain (Ventura et al., 2001). Similarly, researchers have found that the association between maternal weight gain and birth weight remains even after accounting for other factors (Abrams and Selvin, 1995). Although the median weight gain has remained relatively constant since 1989, there has been an increase in the percentage of mothers who gained less than 16 pounds and in the percentage of mothers who gained more than 46 pounds. These changes in the extremes of the weight gain distribution are thought to have had offsetting effects. Based on these observed trends in weight gain, it does not appear that weight gain is driving the increase in the low birth weight rate that has been observed in Los Angeles County and that is shown in Figure 2.1.

Prenatal Care. Although there is a common perception that prenatal care can improve birth outcomes such as birth weight, the empirical evidence is equivocal (Alexander and Korenbrot, 1995; Fiscella 1995; Kramer, 1987; Harris, 1982). Some studies have found beneficial impacts of adequate prenatal care for specific populations, while others have found no effect at all (Olds et al., 1986; McLaughlin et al., 1992; Schlesinger and Kronebusch, 1990; Currie and Gruber, 1994). Data for Los Angeles County show that during the 1990s the percentage of women initiating prenatal care during the first trimester increased

---

[2]California does not collect behavioral risk factors on the birth certificate other than the use of prenatal care. Beginning in 1989, most states began collecting data on maternal smoking, drinking, and weight gain. California, however, has chosen not to collect these data. As such, the information about changes in behavioral risk factors over time is based on national data that exclude California.

from 71 percent in 1991 to 86 percent in 1999. (Estimates are based on the authors' tabulations of birth certificate data for the County.) Furthermore, the percentage of women receiving no prenatal care at any time during pregnancy fell from 1.5 percent to 0.6 percent over the same time period. Although research has not shown conclusively that prenatal care has a beneficial impact on birth weight, there is no evidence to suggest it has a negative impact. As such, the increases in the use of prenatal care in the County during the 1990s cannot explain the observed increase in the percentage of infants being born with low birth weights.

Demographics

As shown in Figure 2.2, there are wide variations in low birth weight birth rates across racial/ethnic groups. In Los Angeles County, the low birth weight birth rate is two times higher among non-Hispanic Black women than among non-Hispanic Whites. Research indicates that the birth weight differences between non-Hispanic Blacks and non-Hispanic Whites remain even after accounting for many other demographic and socioeconomic characteristics (Chomitz et al., 1995; Collins and David, 1990).

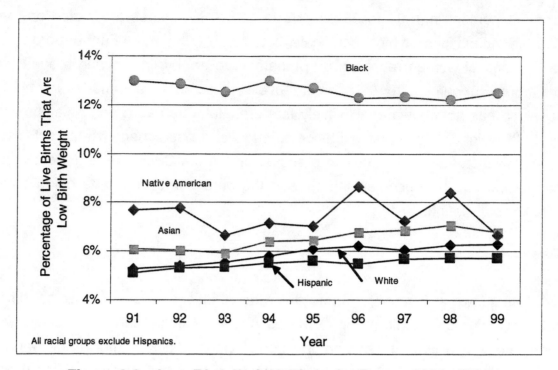

Figure 2.2—Low Birth Weight Births by Race: 1991–1999

Given this trend, if births to non-Hispanic Blacks in Los Angeles County grew as a percentage of all births during the 1990s, then we would have expected to see increases in the percentage of infants born weighing less than 2,500 grams. Although there has been a substantial shift in the demographic composition of the County during the 1990s, the percentage of the population who are non-Hispanic Blacks has actually been falling (as shown in Figure 2.3). Similarly, the percentage of births that were to non-Hispanic Black mothers has fallen during this time period. Furthermore, the percentage of births to Hispanic women has increased from 58 percent in 1991 to 62 percent in 1999, and Hispanics have the *lowest* rate of low birth weight of all racial/ethnic groups. Therefore, it does not appear that demographic shifts in the population of the County can explain the rise in the low birth weight birth rate.

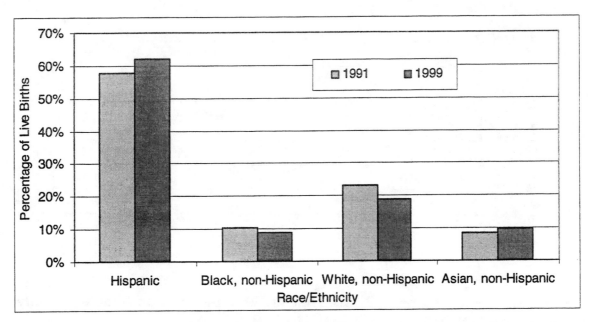

Figure 2.3—Change in Racial/Ethnic Composition of Births in Los Angeles County: 1991–1999

Birth Characteristics

Twins, triplets, and higher-order births tend to be born at much lower weights than singleton births. In Los Angeles County in 1999, the low birth weight rate for multiples was 56 percent, compared to 5 percent for singletons. Furthermore, as shown in Figure 2.4, the share of births that are twins, triplets, or higher order has been growing over the last decade in the County. Moreover, the correlation coefficient between the Countywide low birth weight rate and the percentage of births that are multiples is 0.85, which indicates a strong positive relationship.

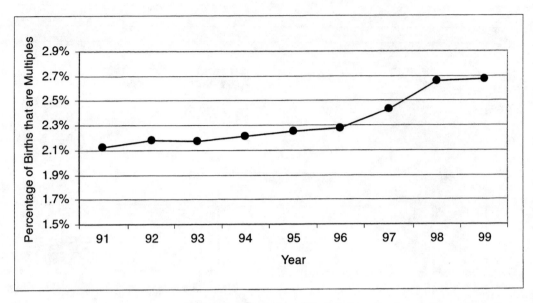

Figure 2.4—Percentage of Births That Are Multiples in Los Angeles County: 1991–1999

The increase in the number of multiple births can help to explain the rise in low birth weight for all births. That is, if the only factor that changed between 1991 and 1999 was the percentage of births that are multiples (a rise from 2.1 percent to 2.7 percent), then the low birth weight birth rate would have increased from 6.1 percent to 6.4 percent. The actual rise was from 6.1 percent to 6.6 percent. Therefore, the increase in multiple births can explain roughly 60 percent ([(6.4–6.1)/(6.6–6.1)]*100) of the rise in low birth weight births.

An alternative way to demonstrate the importance of the rise in multiple births is to examine low birth weight births for births of only one child, i.e., singletons. When considering only singleton births, the low birth weight birth rate remained relatively constant between 1991 and 1999, as shown in Figure 2.5.

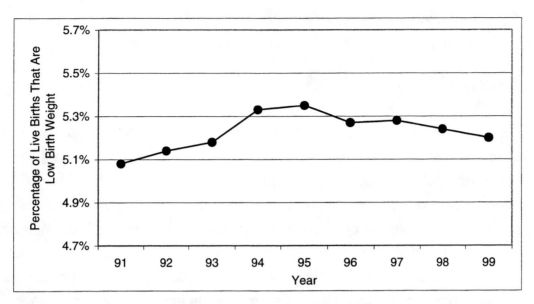

Figure 2.5—Low Birth Weight among Singleton Births in Los Angeles County: 1991–1999

If the rise in multiple births can explain the increase in the low birth weight birth rate, then the natural question to ask is, what is causing the rise in multiple births? The observed increase in multiple births has been attributed to two distinct factors: (1) shifts in the maternal age distribution; and (2) the proliferation of fertility treatments. Since the late 1970s, maternal age at birth has been rising and accounts for approximately one-third of the growth in multiples. Older women are more likely physiologically to have a multiple birth (Martin and Park, 1999). The remainder of the increase likely results from changes in the use of fertility treatments, such as in-vitro fertilization and fertility-enhancing drug therapies, which increase the likelihood of plural births (Martin and Park, 1999).

It is interesting to note that the increase in multiple births has been concentrated among more educated, older, White women, the group most likely to use fertility treatments (Jewell and Yip, 1995). Given this finding, the low-income group targeted by the LTFSS Plan has likely experienced *less* growth in the number of multiple births than the population as a whole. Consequently, we would not expect the low birth weight birth rate among the target group to show as much of an increase as is observed in Figure 2.1. Unfortunately, data on low birth weight births among CalWORKs participants or other participants of the

LTFSS Plan projects are not currently available. Future work will attempt to fill this void by matching birth certificate data with CalWORKs records.

Public Policy

Many of the public policies and programs that have been implemented in an effort to improve birth outcomes have focused on providing pregnant women with adequate nutrition and access to prenatal care. The most notable of such initiatives are the Women, Infants, and Children (WIC) program and the expansion of Medicaid benefits to pregnant women in the late 1980s. While the evidence on the effectiveness of WIC in improving birth outcomes is varied, on balance the results suggest there is a positive effect (Hughes and Simpson, 1995). WIC participants receive food supplements and nutritional education. In addition, they may receive health and social service referrals. Such referrals may play a role in the improved low birth weight birth rates among WIC participants (Devaney, 1992).

In contrast, evaluations of the Medicaid expansions have provided little evidence of improvements in the low birth weight birth rate (Frick and Lantz, 1996). The most comprehensive study does find a statistically significant impact of the expansion of eligibility for health insurance coverage on the rate of low birth weight births, but this impact is relatively small (Currie and Gruber, 1994). However, the study does find a large beneficial impact of the expansions on reducing infant mortality.

PROJECTS TARGETING LOW BIRTH WEIGHT BIRTHS

The results from the evaluations of these programs to improve birth outcomes provide some insight into the potential effects of other programs being implemented in Los Angeles County. Under the LTFSS Plan, two projects are expected to directly affect low birth weight: Project 10—Community Outreach to Increase Access to Health Care, and Project 34—Home Visitation Program. (See Appendix A for a full list of the projects.) Project 10 helps pregnant women gain access to prenatal care and provides additional support services, such as parenting skill training, health education, and breast feeding education. Through home visits by public health nurses, Project 34 will provide parenting education and support and provide referrals to other needed social services to young, first-time pregnant needy CalWORKs participants. These projects expect to improve access to prenatal care and provide valuable information about proper nutrition and the behavioral risk factors associated with low birth weight births. As such, they may be expected to have a beneficial impact on birth weight for the populations they serve; however, based on results from the literature, such effects may be relatively small. Whether such improvements can be detected at the County level partly depends on the scale of the projects. For example, although a small program may be quite successful, the low number of women served will be too few to affect the overall Countywide trend.

In addition to the projects that seek to directly affect low birth weight, numerous projects under the LTFSS Plan are designed to improve access to health care in general: Project 11—Hotline to Resolve Health Care Access Issues, Project 12—Health Care Transportation, and Project 13—Health First. These projects can be expected to have an indirect impact on low birth weight births. Such improvements may come through general improvements in health and greater access to regular preventive health care, but again, these effects are not expected to be very large.

FORECASTS

To try to understand where the County is headed in terms of low birth weight births, we provide some forecasts. The forecasts are developed to predict what would happen in the absence of the LTFSS Plan. We provide three alternative forecasts based on three different modeling assumptions. The first assumption is that the recent and future trends are accurately represented with a linear extrapolation over the period 1994–2000. These assumptions lead to the "medium" estimates shown in Figure 2.6.

The second forecast also assumes that a curvilinear relationship is the most appropriate, but the model is based on data from the entire 1991–2000 period. This model leads to the estimates labeled "low" on Figure 2.6. The third and final forecast is based on the assumption that the leveling off and slight fall between 1998 and 2000 were not representative. Specifically, we assume a linear specification over the 1991–2000 period. The forecast based on these assumptions is labeled "high."

The range of the estimates is less than half a percentage point. The "low" estimate projects the low birth weight birth rate as holding fairly steady at 6.3 percent. The "high" estimate implies a slight increase in the low birth weight birth rate, from 6.3 percent in 2000 to 6.7 percent in 2003. The "medium" estimate is between these two at 6.4 percent.

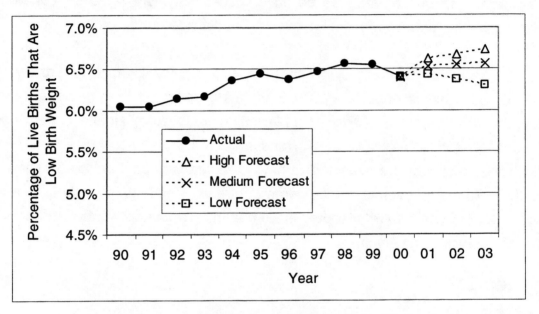

Figure 2.6—Forecasts for Rate of Low Birth Weight Births in Los Angeles County: 2001-2003

As noted previously, children born with a low birth weight face a higher risk of health and developmental problems throughout their childhood. These problems can be very costly, both for the family and for the community. An increased need for medical care represents the most significant cost associated with low birth weight. As evidence, one study has calculated that the incremental cost of low birth weight was $5.4 billion per year nationally in 1988 ($5.9 billion in 2000 dollars), with more than 75 percent of these costs attributed to medical care (Lewit et al., 1995). The remainder includes special education costs, costs of grade repetition, and child care costs. These estimates, however, do not include the costs of relatively rare, but extremely costly, needs, such as long-term care or institutionalization; thus, they may represent a lower bound. Consequently, if the low birth weight birth rate continues to increase, significant additional monetary costs will accrue.

OTHER INDICATORS OF GOOD HEALTH

Unlike the low birth weight indicator, the other indicators used to measure progress toward the goal of good health generally show improvements over the last decade. Table 2.1 reports Countywide estimates for each non-headline indicator, with more-detailed estimates and data sources listed in Appendix B. The infant mortality rate in the County has fallen from 7.72 infant deaths per 1,000 live births in 1991 to 5.95 in 1997. Similarly, the birth rate for girls age 10 to 17 has fallen significantly during the 1990s, from 20.7 in 1991 to 12.5 in 1999. These improvements have been seen across all racial/ethnic groups.

Table 2.1 Nonheadline Indicators for Good Health in Los Angeles County: 1990–1999

Indicator	90	91	92	93	94	95	96	97	98	99
Deaths to babies under 12 months per 1,000 live births		7.7	7.4	7.2	7.0	6.7	5.9	5.9		
Births to women 10–17 per 1,000 women 10–17		20.7	20.0	19.6	19.3	18.7	16.9	15.2	13.8	12.5
Percentage of persons without health insurance	16.2	26.2	26.9	26.1	29.1	28.9	27.5	29.1	30.1	28.8

The percentage of individuals in Los Angeles County who do not have health insurance is the exception, showing a general upward trend since the mid-1980s. This increase in the percentage of people without health insurance can be partly explained by the demographic changes that have occurred in the County. Based on data from the California Department of Finance (CDF), the Hispanic population, which is most likely to be uninsured, has grown from approximately 36 percent of the population to 45 percent between 1989 and 1999.

Throughout the last decade in Los Angeles County, the percentage of Hispanics who are uninsured has been two to three times higher than for non-Hispanic Whites or non-Hispanic Blacks. As a result, the growth in the Hispanic population can account for all of the rise in the proportion of people without health insurance. Holding the composition of the population constant at 1989 levels, the percentage uninsured would have stayed virtually unchanged over the 1990s, as shown in Figure 2.7. Instead, the percentage uninsured increased over much of the period. This indicates that programs designed to improve access to health care need to be targeted most heavily toward Hispanics.

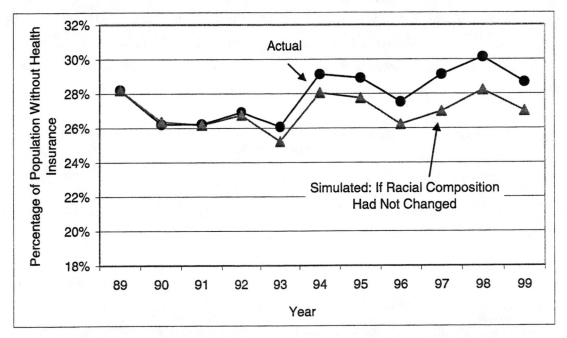

Figure 2.7—People without Health Insurance If Racial/Ethnic Composition Had Not Changed in Los Angeles County: 1989–1999

CONCLUSIONS

As shown above, the percentage of low birth weight infants in Los Angeles County has been increasing during the 1990s; this upward trend is also seen in the rest of California and the nation as a whole. Of the potential explanations for this increase—maternal risk factors (such as smoking, drinking, and low maternal weight gain), demographic characteristics and characteristics of birth, and changes in public policy—we find that characteristics of birth—in particular, increases in the number of multiple births—is the primary explanatory factor. Twelve of the LTFSS Plan projects are expected to have an impact on the low birth weight birth rate, two of them directly. High, low, and medium forecasts out to 2003 are projected to be 6.7, 6.3, and 6.4 percent, respectively. If the low birth weight birth rate continues to increase, significant additional monetary costs will accrue, mostly for medical care. With the exception of the percentage of persons without health insurance, the other indicators of good health have improved over the last decade.

3. SAFETY AND SURVIVAL: DOMESTIC VIOLENCE ARRESTS

Within the safety and survival outcome area, the LTFSS Plan specified five indicators: (1) domestic violence arrests, (2) child placement in out-of-home care, (3) juvenile probation violations, (4) successful/minor family reunification after out-of-home care, and (5) youth arrests for violent crimes. A sixth indicator, homicides, was added to this outcome area by the Evaluation Design Workgroup (Hedderson and Schoeni, 2001). Successful/minor family reunification after out-of-home care was placed on the Data Development Agenda. The rate of domestic violence arrests was chosen as the headline indicator because it is compelling, because it is easily understood, and because data are available. The operational definition is the number of arrests per 100,000 people age 18 and over.

ESTABLISHING THE BASELINE

Figure 3.1 shows the domestic violence arrest rate for Los Angeles County from 1988 to 1998. The data contain arrests for violation of California Penal Code 273.5 (a) "Willful infliction of corporal injury upon spouse/cohabitant" (Herbert, 1999). Although this is a felony offense, the most serious domestic violence incidents, those resulting in death, are not included, because they are charged as homicides. According to these data, between 1988 and 1998, arrests for this domestic violence offense have been increasing in the County. Over this time period, the total number of arrests per year increased 38 percent, from 12,435 to 17,190 (data not shown). Because the population grew as well, the domestic violence arrest rate grew at a slightly slower rate, from 198 to 252 arrests per 100,000 between 1988 and 1998 (as shown in the figure). This upward trend in the arrest rate is not unique to Los Angeles County; it has been observed for the rest of the state as well (Table B.5).

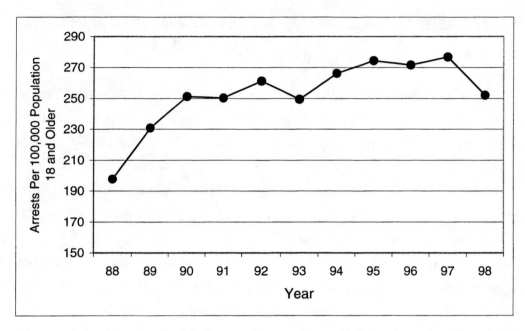

**Figure 3.1—Domestic Violence Arrest Rate in Los Angeles County:
1988–1998**

THE STORY BEHIND THE BASELINE

One particular challenge for communities seeking to understand the extent of the problem locally is identifying a source of data that can be used to count and describe domestic violence incidents. Often, the only available source of this information is arrest data from local law enforcement agencies. While these data are certainly valuable, they do not directly capture domestic violence in local communities. In general, victimization surveys and homicide data are regarded as less biased sources of information about domestic violence incidents than arrest data. Surveys that are representative of the general public capture both those who are willing and those who are unwilling to report their abuse to police or other agencies, and these data are not influenced by police policies or record-keeping (Canton and Lynch, 2000). Homicide is widely regarded as the best reported violent crime; thus, homicide data serve as a good indicator of the level of violence in a community; as homicides go up, assaults go up, and as homicides go down, assaults go down. Thus, domestic violence homicide data are seen as a good source of information about the trends in domestic violence assaults (Reiss and Roth, 1993).

Unfortunately, victimization survey data are not available specifically for the County, and domestic violence homicide data are not readily available in a published source. Domestic violence arrest data are available for the County, but careful consideration must be given to the limitations of this data source. In general, there are three influences on law enforcement data: (1) domestic violence incidents occurring in a community, (2) the willingness of victims or others to report these incidents to police, and (3) police behavior once the police receive a report of an incident. Specifically, when the actual number of incidents occurring in the community increases, all things being equal, we would expect arrests to increase. Likewise, even if the number of incidents remains constant, if more victims and community residents are willing to call police about domestic violence, we would expect arrests to increase. Finally, even if the actual level of domestic violence incidents and reporting to police remain the same, if police departments institute more-stringent policies requiring arrests when police find probable cause to do so, the arrest rate will increase.

Of course, it is likely that all three of these factors interact with one another. For example, many mandatory arrest policies are adopted because of the expectation that increased arrests will reduce the level of actual incidents in a community (Sherman, 1992). In addition, increased arrests may lead to increases in reporting to police if, as a result, victims and community members come to view domestic violence as criminal behavior and police officers as more willing to respond to these incidents (Frisch and Caruso, 1992). Under both of these circumstances, we would observe an increase in the domestic violence arrest rate, but the actual level of domestic violence incidents would be on the decline. While these expectations may seem reasonable, the available research evidence is mixed about whether increased arrests reduce the number of domestic violence incidents (Sherman, 1992; Garner and Maxwell, 2000) and has not yet examined whether increased arrests increase rates of reporting to police.

Consequently, how we interpret changes in domestic violence arrest data depends very heavily on which of these three influences we believe these data most closely measure. For example, if the arrest rate is driven by changes in the number of domestic violence incidents, then the increases observed during the

1990s are quite troubling. In contrast, if the changes in the arrest rate reflect changes in people's willingness to report incidents to police or changes in police practice, then the observed increases could be considered improvements.

The criminal justice literature provides some insight into the factors that affect each of these three influences on domestic violence arrests. These factors include victimization, demographics, income level, and public policy. Each is discussed below.

Victimization

Victimization refers to the actual incidence of domestic violence. Data on victimization are only available at the national level. As shown in Figure 3.2, according to data from the National Crime Victimization Survey (NCVS), domestic violence victimization has been on the decline since 1993 (Rennison, 2001).

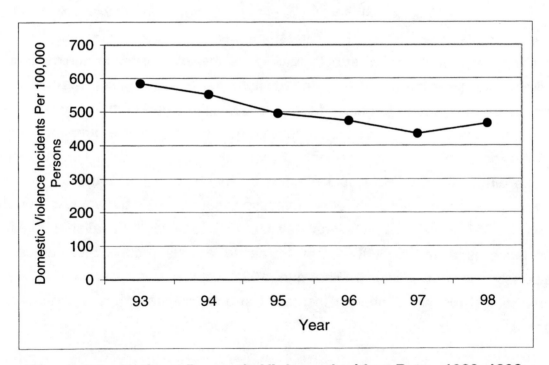

Figure 3.2—National Domestic Violence Incident Rate: 1993–1998

Demographics

Age has been found to be associated with domestic violence incidents. Like other violent crimes, violence toward intimate partners is more common among the young (Straus and Gelles, 1990). According to the NCVS, females between the ages of 16 and 24 are most at risk for non-lethal domestic violence (Greenfeld et al., 1998). In contrast, researchers have not found age to be an important influence on the reporting of domestic violence victims (Hutchison, 1998; Bachman and Coker, 1995; Johnson, 1990). Furthermore, domestic violence researchers do not yet understand the impact of age of victims or offenders on the probability of arrest. General research on police behavior is inconclusive on whether age matters for arrest (Brooks, 1997).

Taken together, these results suggest that if the age distribution in the County is becoming younger, then the higher prevalence of domestic violence among young adults could explain some of the observed increase in the domestic violence arrest rate. However, the population of adults in Los Angeles County has become older during this time period, as shown in Figure 3.3. (Estimates in Figure 3.3 are from the CDF.) The percentage of the population age 18 to 24 fell from 18 percent in 1988 to 12 percent in 1998. Similarly, the population age 25 to 34 also declined. Following national trends, the age distribution in the County shifted upwards, showing a growth in the population age 35 to 55. As such, changes in the age distribution of the population in the County do not explain the observed changes in the arrest rate for domestic violence.

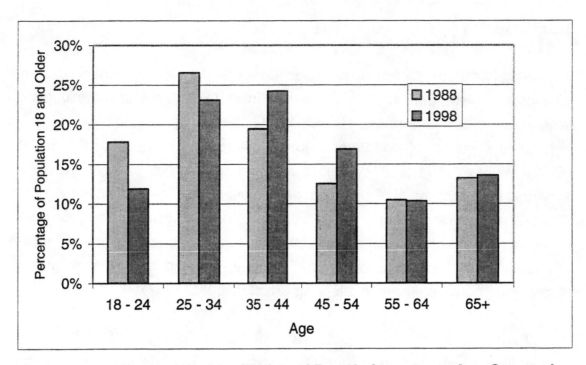

Figure 3.3—Changes in Distribution of Population across Age Groups in Los Angeles County: 1988–1998

Race is another factor associated with domestic violence incidents. African Americans tend to suffer domestic violence at a rate higher than Whites (Straus, Gelles, and Steinmetz, 1980; Greenfeld et al., 1998; Tjaden and Thoennes, 2000). The National Violence Against Women Survey finds that, when compared to other races, both male and female American Indian/Alaska Natives experience domestic violence at an even higher rate than African Americans (Tjaden and Thoennes, 2000).[1] At this time, there is not enough consistent evidence to determine whether Hispanics are at a greater or lesser risk of domestic violence than non-Hispanics (Greenfeld et al., 1998; Tjaden and Thoennes, 2000).

With regard to the likelihood of reporting domestic violence to police and the likelihood of police arrests, there is no consensus in the literature on whether race makes a difference (Felson et al., 1999; Brooks, 1997; Fyfe, Klinger, and Flavin, 1997; Klinger, 1996; Bachman and Coker, 1995; Kantor and Straus,

---

[1]American Indian/Alaska Natives tend to be included in the "Other Races" category in publications of findings from other surveys.

1990; Smith and Klein, 1984; Smith and Visher, 1981; Lundman et al., 1978; Black and Reiss, 1970).

The data on arrests in Los Angeles County are not broken down by race. As such, we must rely on results based on national surveys to try to understand what has caused the observed increase in the domestic violence arrest rate in the County. The racial composition of the population in the County changed during this time. As shown in Figure 3.4, between 1988 and 1998, the population of Hispanics grew from 36 percent to 44 percent of the total. (Estimates are based on data from the March Current Population Survey, CPS.) In contrast, the percentage of non-Hispanic Whites fell from 43 percent to 34 percent, while the percentage of the population who are non-Hispanic Blacks fell slightly. Because African Americans have higher rates of domestic violence, the decline in their population does not appear to explain the observed increase in arrests. Because little is known about the relationship between Hispanic ethnicity and domestic violence, it is difficult to determine whether the changes in the racial composition of Los Angeles County have contributed to the increases in the domestic violence arrest rate we saw in Figure 3.1.

Regarding victim reporting in general, there is substantial evidence that domestic violence is an underreported offense. Estimates range from a low of around 7 percent of all physical assault incidents in the National Family Violence Survey (Kantor and Straus, 1990) to 50 percent in the NCVS (Greenfeld et al., 1998). Very little research yet exists on the factors that influence victim reporting. It is reasonable to expect that immigrants and non-English speaking victims and community members may be more reluctant to report domestic violence to police than other groups. However, adequate research has not yet been undertaken to quantify the underreporting of these groups relative to others.

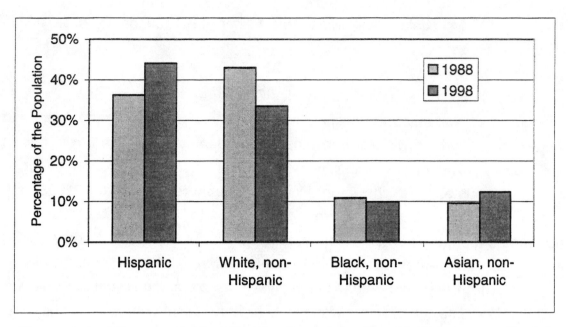

Figure 3.4—Changes in the Distribution of the Population across Racial Groups in Los Angeles County: 1988–1998

Income Level

Previous research provides some evidence that socioeconomic status is related to domestic violence incidents. Victimization surveys have shown that income has an impact on domestic violence in that the poor are more likely to disclose this form of violence than the more well-to-do (Greenfeld et al., 1998; Straus and Gelles, 1990). The rate continues to decrease with each successive income level. In contrast, limited evidence suggests victim or household income does not influence the reporting of violence in the NCVS survey (Bachman and Coker, 1995).

Given these findings, changes in the poverty rate in Los Angeles County could be expected to impact the incidence of domestic violence. Data from the CPS that are reported in the subsequent chapter (Chapter 4) show that during the early 1990s, the poverty rate increased and then, in the latter part of the decade, declined, leaving poverty at approximately the same level in 1988 and 1998. This pattern is not consistent with the changes in the domestic violence arrest rate. Thus, changes in income do not appear to help explain the observed increases in the domestic violence arrest rate.

Public Policy

Over the last 20 years, there has been an increasing awareness of the complexity, potential severity, and widespread nature of domestic violence. Consequently, many states, including California, have enacted legislation that specifically penalizes domestic violence, expands police arrest powers, and establishes new policies that either encourage or require arrest in domestic violence incidents. Because of the numerous efforts at the national, state, and local level to encourage arrest for domestic violence offenses, increases in arrest rates are often considered a positive outcome reflecting improvement of police practice. In fact, recent increases in arrest rates are most commonly interpreted by domestic violence researchers as the result of changes in police policies and practice rather than in underlying domestic violence incidents (Healey, Smith, and O'Sullivan, 1998; Buzawa, Austin, and Buzawa, 1995; Frisch and Caruso, 1992).

There is considerable evidence that arrest rates are responsive to the adoption of police training and new domestic violence policies, either locally or at a state level. For example, after the adoption of statewide pro-arrest policies in Massachusetts, there was a fivefold increase in the share of reports resulting in arrest (Mignon and Holmes, 1995) and a near doubling over a ten-year period in the state of Maryland (Garner et al., 1999).

During and immediately prior to the time period we have data for (1990 to 1998), a number of changes were initiated in California that are specifically targeted toward increasing police use of arrest in domestic violence situations. In 1986, legislation was adopted that required police to receive specialized training in responding to domestic violence calls and that instructed them to treat violence between intimates as criminal conduct. In 1995, other legislation required police officers to receive additional training every two years on domestic violence policies and procedures. During that same year, all California law enforcement agencies were required to adopt written policies encouraging the use of arrest in domestic violence cases (Herbert, 1999). In addition to these legislative efforts, many local organizations have been established to address domestic violence, including improving police response. In fact, since the passage of the Violence Against Women Act of 1994, the federal "Grants to Encourage Arrest Policies Program" has provided millions of dollars to organizations seeking to increase arrests of domestic violence offenders within the state.

These multiple policy and program changes, combined with the findings of other studies, suggest that the increasing trend in the domestic violence arrest rate observed within the County results from changes in public policy rather than from an actual increase in violence. Unfortunately, because of the lack of appropriate data, it is impossible to know for certain.

PROJECTS TARGETING DOMESTIC VIOLENCE

The criminal justice research literature can be used to make predictions about the potential impacts of the LTFSS Plan. Specifically, two projects under the LTFSS Plan seek to directly impact domestic violence in the County: Project 27—DART/STOP for CalWORKs Families, and Project 28—Domestic Violence Prevention. Both LTFSS Plan projects focus on preventing domestic violence incidents.

The Los Angeles Police Department (LAPD) and the Los Angeles County Sheriff's Department have established emergency response teams in some areas to respond to domestic violence. Project 27 would link the existing CalWORKs Domestic Violence Program with the LAPD and Sheriff's Department response teams to facilitate access to services for CalWORKs participants who are victims of domestic violence.

Project 28 will develop a domestic violence risk assessment tool for use with CalWORKs participants. The assessment is intended to help determine individual risk of violence by an intimate partner. Participants will also be provided information about what to do if they are abused. In addition, the project will develop and distribute a domestic violence curriculum for teenagers in an effort to identify and prevent domestic violence among the young.

In addition to the projects that focus directly on domestic violence, other projects that improve economic well-being may have an indirect impact on the incidence of domestic violence. As noted previously, research shows that domestic violence is more common among lower-income women. As such, programs that improve income would be expected to reduce the number of domestic violence incidents in the County. Moreover, in 1998 the Board approved spending $12 million annually on domestic violence services to CalWORKs families, which may also influence observed trends.

FORECASTS

Three forecasts are provided here based on three different assumptions (as shown in Figure 3.5). The forecasts are developed to predict what would happen in the absence of the LTFSS Plan. The first forecast—"medium"—assumes a linear trend from 1993 to 2000. The second forecast—"low"—is based on a curvilinear trend over the entire period 1988 to 2000. The third forecast—"high"—is based on a linear relationship fit over the entire period 1988 to 2000.

The "medium" estimate implies that the arrest rate will increase from its 2000 level, but will remain well below its level of the late 1990s. With this forecast, the arrest rate would reach 214.3 per 1000,000 of the population over 18 in 2003. The "low" estimate has arrest rates continuing to drop, reaching 143.2 in 2003. Finally, the "high" estimate has arrest rates returning to their long-term levels, reaching 258.0 in 2003.

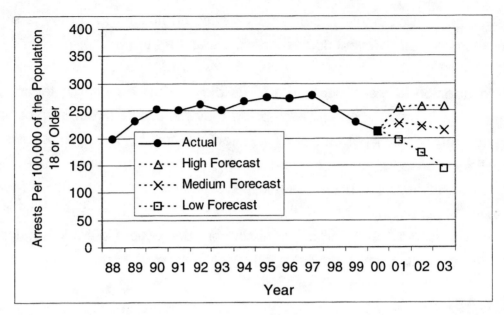

Figure 3.5—Forecasts for Domestic Violence Arrests in Los Angeles County: 2001–2003

Although we believe the baseline trend in domestic violence arrests represents improvements since 1988, there is still more that can be done. Decreasing the actual number of domestic violence incidents is the overarching societal goal. In addition to the obvious human costs associated with domestic violence, there are significant monetary costs. These costs include medical and mental health care, temporary housing, and other social services. Consequently, reducing the incidence of domestic violence below the level that might occur in the absence of the LTFSS Plan not only improves public safety but also could reduce costs.

OTHER INDICATORS OF SAFETY AND SURVIVAL

Table 3.1 reports Countywide estimates for each non-headline indicator, with more detailed estimates and data sources listed in Appendix B. The observed trends in the other indicators of safety and survival are consistent with the story that the increase in domestic violence arrests reflects changes in police behavior rather than an increase in the actual number of domestic violence incidents in the community. That is, all other indicators have shown improvements in recent years. The homicide rate (number of homicides per 100,000 population), the youth arrest rate for violent crimes (number of arrests per 100,000 youth), and the child placement in out-of-home care (number of placements per 1,000 children) have fallen considerably during the 1990s.

As discussed above, homicide rates are considered a good indicator of violent crime trends in communities. In part, this reflects the fact that homicides are more likely to be reported to police than domestic violence incidents. As a result, it is generally thought that changes in homicides are more reflective of changes in the number of actual incidents occurring than in police behavior once an incident is reported. Taken together, the indicators of safety and survival show improvements over the last decade. These trends suggest that changes in police behavior more than changes in the actual number of domestic violence incidents explain the upward trend in arrests for domestic violence.

Table 3.1 Nonheadline Indicators for Safety and Survival in Los Angeles County: 1990–1999

Indicator	90	91	92	93	94	95	96	97	98	99
Child placement in out-of-home care per 1,000 children (0-18)	4.6	4.4	4.4	4.8	4.5	4.5	5.2	4.7	3.4	3.2
Youth arrests for violent crime per 100,000 children under 18	1064	949	913	818	773	724	647	591	536	
Homicides per 100,000 persons	21.4	22.5	22.8	22.0	19.4	18.8	15.8	13.4	10.6	9.5

CONCLUSIONS

As shown above, domestic violence arrests have increased in Los Angeles County from 1988 to 1998, rising from 198 arrests per 100,000 people over the age of 18 to 252; this upward trend is also seen in the rest of California. Of the potential explanations for this increase—victimization, demographics, income level, and changes in public policy—changes in public policy—in particular, changes in police behavior leading to more arrests—appear to be the driving factor. Although there is no California- or County-specific evidence on actual incidents of domestic violence (victimization), national trends indicate a decline in such incidents since 1993 and suggest that domestic violence incidence may also be in decline in the County. Thus, the increase in domestic violence arrests resulting from changes in police behavior can be viewed as an improvement. Of the 18 projects that are expected to have an impact on domestic violence incidents, two will affect it directly. High, medium, and low forecasts out to 2003 are projected to be 305, 222, and 186 arrests per 100,000 people over the age of 18, respectively. Although we believe the baseline trend in domestic violence arrests represents improvements since 1998, more can still be done; reducing the incidence of domestic violence below its 1998 level would improve public safety and could reduce costs. All other indicators of safety and survival have shown improvements in recent years, consistent with the story that an increase in domestic violence arrests reflects changes in police behavior rather than an increase in the actual number of domestic violence incidents in the community.

4. ECONOMIC WELL-BEING: ANNUAL INCOME UNDER POVERTY LEVEL

Within the economic well-being outcome area, the LTFSS Plan specified six indicators: (1) adults employed by quarter, (2) annual income under poverty level, (3) access to transportation, (4) percentage of family income used for housing, (5) adults earning a living wage, and (6) homeless within prior 24 months. Access to transportation, adults earning a living wage, and homeless within prior 24 months were placed on the Data Development Agenda. Annual income under poverty level was chosen as the headline indicator. Poverty is a widely used measure of economic well-being, and the data are readily available. In fact, data on poverty are so readily available that we can examine the poverty rate in Los Angeles County in a much broader context, going back 25 years. The poverty rate is defined as the percentage of people living in families whose income is below the federal poverty threshold.

ESTABLISHING THE BASELINE

The poverty rate has fluctuated throughout the past 25 years. In the late 1970s, roughly 12 percent of Angelenos lived in poverty, but this rate increased rapidly during the 1981–1984 period (as shown in Figure 4.1). After falling back to about 13 percent in 1986/1987, the rate experienced a large, steady increase over the subsequent eight years, reaching almost 25 percent in 1994.

The poverty rate has declined rapidly in the County since the mid-1990s. In 1999 (the year for which the latest data are available), 17 percent of Angelenos lived in families in which their income was below the poverty level given the size of their family. This represents a drop from 25 percent in 1994, with most of the gains occurring between 1997 and 1999.

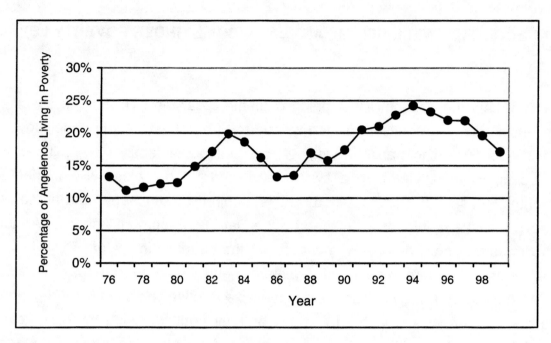

Figure 4.1—Annual Income under Poverty Level in Los Angeles County: 1976–1999

Despite the substantial improvements since 1994, the long-run trend over the entire 25-year period for which data are available has been toward higher poverty. The recent decline would have to continue for several more years before poverty reached the level of 11–13 percent that existed in the late 1970s.

THE STORY BEHIND THE BASELINE

When we seek to understand the story behind annual income under poverty baseline, the research points to three key factors: (1) the macroeconomy, (2) demographics, and (3) changes in poverty and welfare policy. Each is discussed below.

Macroeconomy

The factor that most powerfully influences poverty is the macroeconomy. A large number of studies have demonstrated that when the economy is growing and robust, poverty falls. This pattern was particularly true in the 1970s, and the prevailing evidence suggests that the economic expansion of the 1990s has had a significant effect in reducing poverty.[1]

Figure 4.2 plots the unemployment rate over time for Los Angeles County, all of California, and the nation as whole. (Unemployment rate estimates were obtained from the California Labor Market Information Division of the Employment Development Department, EDD.) The longest economic expansion in the history of our nation occurred during the 1990s, with an unemployment rate of 4.0 percent in 2000. Nationally, virtually all groups benefited from the robust economy, with the unemployment rate for Blacks and Hispanics at their lowest levels since the numbers began to be estimated (Council of Economic Advisers, 1999).

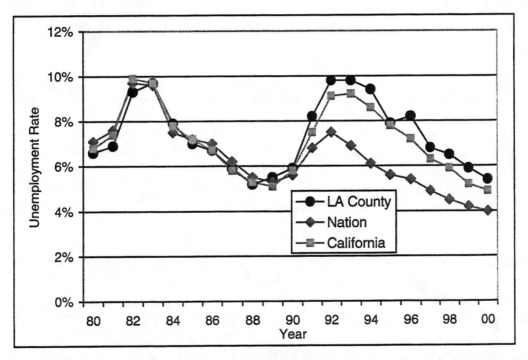

Figure 4.2—Unemployment Rates for the Nation, for California, and for Los Angeles County: 1980–2000

---

[1]The latest evidence is from Blank (2000) and Haveman and Schwabish (1999). Earlier studies include Blank (1993) and Blank and Blinder (1986).

Figure 4.2 also shows that the labor market has improved substantially in the County during the 1990s. However, the improvements began later, and the recession of the early 1990s was much deeper and more prolonged than in the nation. During the decade of the 1980s, the unemployment rate in the County mirrored the rate in the nation as a whole. By 1994, the unemployment rate in the County was roughly 3 percentage points higher than in the nation. Although this gap has shrunk, the unemployment rate in 1999 (the year of the latest available data on poverty) remained almost 2 percentage points higher in the County than in the nation as a whole—5.9 percent versus 4.0 percent.

The empirical evidence suggests that the macroeconomy is an important driver of poverty in Los Angeles County as well, as shown in Figure 4.3. When unemployment rose during the recession of the early 1990s, so too did poverty. And when the labor market began to expand in the mid-1990s, the poverty rate fell.

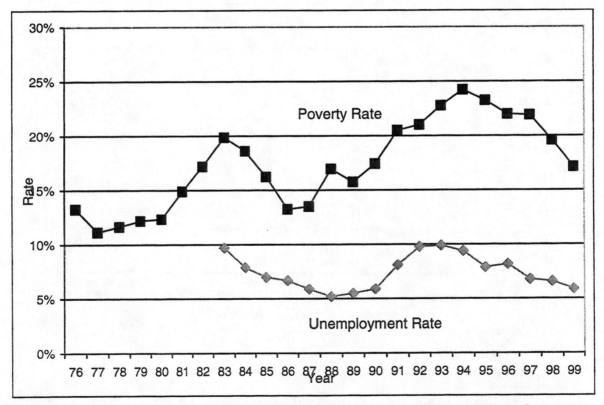

Figure 4.3—Unemployment Rate and Poverty Rate in Los Angeles County: 1976–1999

The research literature finds that a 1 percentage point decline in the unemployment rate leads to at most a 0.75 percentage point decline in the poverty rate. Between 1993 and 1999, the unemployment rate fell by 4.0 percentage points in the County, from 9.9 percent to 5.9 percent. The research literature implies that one would have expected poverty to fall by no more than 3 percentage points during this period (Blank, 2000; Haveman and Schwabish, 1999). However, the decline in poverty was much larger, from 22.7 percent to 17.1 percent, or 5.6 percentage points. Therefore, the economic expansion can account for just over half (54 percent) of the improvement in poverty in the second half of the 1990s. One must look to other factors to explain the remainder of the improvement.

Demographics

The changing demographic landscape in the County is a leading candidate to help explain the observed changes in poverty. Poverty is much more prevalent among Hispanics and non-Hispanic Blacks than Whites, in part because of relatively low levels of education, especially among Hispanics. For each of the major racial/ethnic groups, Figure 4.4 shows the lowest annual poverty rates for the three business cycles since 1976. In 1999, 25.6 percent of Hispanics and 19.7 percent of non-Hispanic Blacks in the County lived in poverty, while just 7.4 percent of non-Hispanic Whites were poor. Moreover, these gaps among racial/ethnic groups have been large throughout the period for which data are available.

The racial/ethnic composition of the population has changed dramatically within the past 25 years. Hispanics accounted for 23 percent of the population in 1976, but now they account for 45 percent. Non-Hispanic Whites now account for 35 percent of Angelenos, down from 58 percent in 1976. The share of the population that is non-Hispanic Black has fallen from 14 percent to 8 percent during this same period. (Estimates are based on the authors' tabulations of the March CPS.)

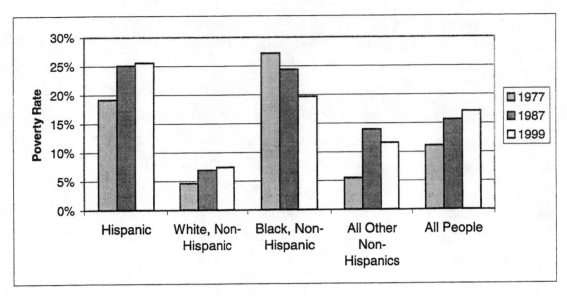

Figure 4.4—Poverty Rate by Race/Ethnicity in Los Angeles County: 1977, 1987, and 1999

The large gaps in poverty among racial/ethnic groups, along with the dramatic change in the racial/ethnic composition, can explain most of the long-run increase in the County's overall poverty rate. To demonstrate this relationship, Figure 4.5 displays the actual poverty rate in each year 1976 to 1999, along with the poverty rate that would have existed had the racial/ethnic composition not changed since 1976. We find that changes in racial/ethnic composition can explain most of the long-run rise in the poverty rate in Los Angeles County. That is, after adjusting for changes in racial/ethnic composition, the poverty rate in 1999 is similar to the rate that existed in the late 1970s.

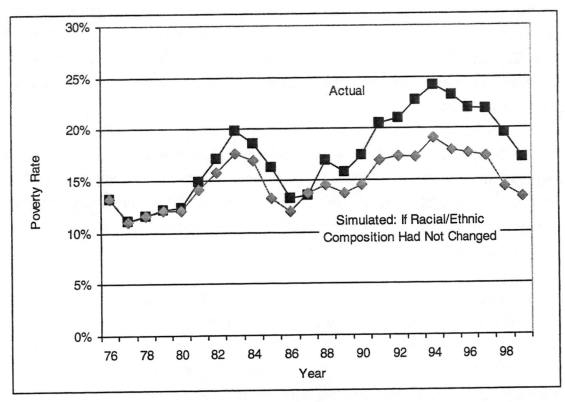

**Figure 4.5—Poverty Rate in Los Angeles County If Racial/Ethnic
Composition Had Not Changed: 1976–1999**

How much of the decline since 1993 can be explained by the combination
of the economic expansion and changes in the racial/ethnic composition of the
population?   As described earlier in this chapter, the economic expansion
accounted for (at most) a 3 percentage point decline in poverty. Had the poverty
rates for each racial/ethnic group remained the same from 1993 to 1999 and
only the composition of the population changed, the poverty rate would have
fallen by 0.38 percentage points. Poverty actually declined from 22.7 percent to
17.1 percent, or 5.6 percentage points, from 1983–1999.   Therefore, the
combined effects of the economic expansion and changes in demographic
composition can account for about 60 percent of the decline in poverty
((3.0+0.36)/5.6)).

Public Policy

Poverty and welfare policy can also play an important role in alleviating
poverty. Assistance in the form of cash raises the income of the poor. The most

common forms of cash assistance are CalWORKs and Supplemental Security Income (SSI). Families can also receive non-cash assistance in the form of Food Stamps, Medicaid, public housing, rental subsidies, and energy assistance. However, these transfers are not directly included in the official Census Bureau calculations of poverty.

Welfare policy has changed dramatically in the 1990s, with an increased emphasis on work participation. Various policies have been implemented to support work, including child care subsidies and health insurance coverage for working families. Moreover, sanctions have been adopted that are placed on families who do not meet certain work requirements.

The hope is that the work-focused policies will increase work participation and skill accumulation, eventually allowing families to move out of poverty by increasing their labor market earnings. The evidence from a number of studies suggests that these policies do in fact increase employment. However, in terms of poverty, only a few initiatives, the initiatives providing the most comprehensive set of employment incentives and work supports, have been effective in reducing poverty (Blank, 2000).

The minimum wage is another policy tool that has the ability to reduce poverty, and the national minimum wage was increased four times in the 1990s, from $3.35 per hour at the beginning of 1990 to $5.15 in 1997. The minimum wage increases have helped low-income families disproportionately. Nationally, among people earning between $4.25 and $5.15 per hour just prior to the increase in the minimum wage in 1997, 71 percent were adults, and most were living in low-income families (Council of Economic Advisors, 1999). The California minimum wage, which increased to $6.25 in 2001 and which will increase to $6.75 in 2002, is higher than the current $5.15 set at the federal level. The concern with increases in the minimum wage is that it may cause reductions in employment among low-income workers because employers hire fewer workers when facing higher wages; however, the research in supporting such arguments is mixed.

The Earned Income Tax Credit (EITC) is an important policy that attempts to achieve the goal of work participation by providing a wage subsidy for low-wage workers, primarily workers with children. The EITC has expanded tremendously, and today more money is spent on the EITC than Temporary Assistance for Needy Families (TANF). In 1998, a single mother with two children could receive a maximum EITC credit of $3,756 per year. Therefore, a full-time worker with two children and earning the minimum wage would have income just above the poverty line, once the EITC was factored in (Blank, 2000). Studies have found that the EITC causes an increase in labor market participation of single mothers (Dickert, House, and Scholz, 1995; Eissa and Liebman, 1996; Meyer and Rosenbaum, 1998), which may, in turn, reduce poverty. Then again, for married women, the evidence suggests that EITC expansions in 1986, 1990, and 1993 reduced labor force participation by about 1 percentage point (Eissa and Hoynes, 1998). Estimates from the Census Bureau show that the EITC removed 4.3 million persons from poverty in 1997 (U.S. Bureau of the Census, 1998). However, the standard definition of poverty used by the Bureau of the Census, which is the one used in this report, does not include EITC in the calculation of poverty.

Figure 4.6 displays the employment rate for 1976 to 1999 among Angelenos on CalWORKs in the given year. (Specifically, the employment estimate is the share of 18–61-year-olds living in a family receiving CalWORKs at any time during the year and who were employed at some time during the year.) The CalWORKs participants experienced large increases in employment in the late 1990s. National data show a similar trend. Studies have attempted to determine whether the rise is accounted for by the economic expansion or by the changes in welfare and poverty policy. The general consensus is that both factors have played an important role (Blank, 2000).

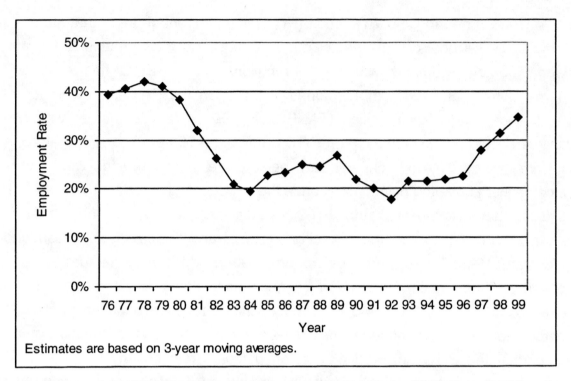

Figure 4.6—Employment Rate among 18–61-Year-Olds Enrolled in CalWORKs in Los Angeles County: 1976–1999

PROJECTS TARGETING POVERTY

Eighteen of the 46 LTFSS Plan projects intend to affect poverty. (See Appendix A for a complete list of projects.) The strategy of many of these projects is to promote self-sustaining employment that will then generate enough income to move families out of poverty and make them independent of government cash assistance. Here, we briefly describe the two largest projects (in terms of dollars allocated) that target poverty. Project 38—Multi-Disciplinary Family Inventory and Case Planning—will have each CalWORKs participant engage in a family inventory, where the family's strengths and needs will be assessed, including the family's involvement with County Departments other than the Department of Public Social Services (DPSS), including the Department of Probation and the Department of Children and Family Services (DCFS). $7.0 million is allocated to Project 38 during the five-year LTFSS Plan period. Project 1 is an expansion of the CalWORKs Welfare-to-Work Strategy, with $4.0 million in funding for the five years. The project builds on the Greater Avenues for

Independence (GAIN) program, while seeking to connect pre-employment and post-employment services more effectively.

FORECASTS

Three forecasts are displayed on Figure 4.7. The forecasts are developed to predict what would happen in the absence of the LTFSS Plan. For all three forecasts presented, the driving factor is the strength of the economy as represented by the unemployment rate. First, recall that the latest measurement of poverty is for 1999. However, the unemployment rate for the County has been measured as recently as July 2001. Therefore, we can use the historical relationship between the unemployment rate and the poverty rate, along with the actual unemployment rate in 2000 and (July) 2001 to make a prediction of poverty in 2000 and 2001. We then extend the predictions of the poverty rate into the future based on alternative predictions of the economy (i.e., the unemployment rate).

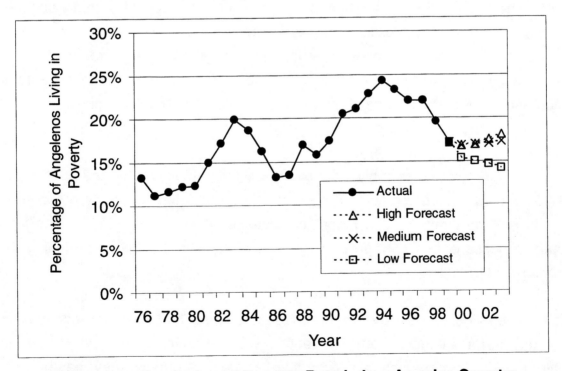

Figure 4.7—Prediction of Poverty Rate in Los Angeles County: 2000–2003

The medium estimates are based on the assumption that the unemployment rate will continue to increase slowly, so that by 2003 the rate is 6.0. The unemployment rate is translated into a change in the poverty rate based on estimates in the research literature, which suggest that a one percentage point increase in the unemployment rate translates into (at most) 0.7 percentage points higher poverty.

The "low" prediction assumes that the economy will expand slightly (i.e., the unemployment rate will fall to 4.7 by 2003, which was roughly the national rate in July 2001). Moreover, it is assumed that there will be additional declines in poverty consistent with the large unexplained declines in poverty that have occurred in the past 4–5 years. That is, the fall in poverty between 1994 and 1999 is greater than can be explained by the fall in unemployment. Therefore, we assume that this unexplained portion will continue to place downward pressure on poverty.

The "high" estimates are based on the exact same approach that was used to make the "medium" estimates, except that a more pessimistic forecast is made for the economy. Instead of the unemployment rate increasing to 6.0 percent by 2003, it is assumed that the rate increases to 7.2, with an annual increase of 0.8 percentage points between 2001 and 2003, similar to the increase in the last recession.

All three estimates imply that poverty will fall between 1999 and 2000, from 17.9 percent to as much as 15.9 percent. The low estimates imply a continual fall in poverty through 2003, reaching a rate of 14 percent in 2003. The less optimistic scenarios imply poverty rising beginning in 2001 and reaching 18 percent in 2003.

The evidence discussed in this chapter suggests that the macroeconomy is the driving force behind short-term variations in the poverty rate. While there is little that LTFSS programs can do to alter the macroeconomy, they may be able to dampen the effects of economic downturns. In the absence of the LTFSS, the "high" forecast shows an increase in the poverty rate starting in 2001. The difficulties associated with increased poverty are felt at both the family and community level. For the County, an increase in the poverty rate will likely lead to increased expenditures on social services as more families become eligible for services and also have greater needs. At the same time, tax revenues will fall, since fewer people will be working and will have less disposable income to spend. As a result, the County may incur significant costs when the poverty rate increases.

OTHER INDICATORS OF ECONOMIC WELL-BEING

In addition to poverty, data are available for the percentage of adults employed and the percentage of income used for housing. Table 4.1 reports estimates for these non-headline indicators, with more-detailed estimates reported in Appendix B. Adults employed is defined as the percentage of adults 18–61 who were employed at any point during the calendar year.[2] Housing costs as a percentage of income are measured as the ratio of the average spending on all housing costs to average household income. Housing costs include the cost of electricity, gas, fuel, oil, garbage pickup, water and sewage, real estate taxes, property insurance, condo fees, land or site rent, and mortgage payments. The remaining three of the six indicators of economic well-being are on the Data Development Agenda.

Employment rate and housing costs as a percentage of income follow trends similar to poverty. That is, as the economy grew in the mid- to late 1990s, the employment rate in the County also increased. Between 1993—the peak of the recession—and 1999—the most recent annual data—employment rose from 72.5 percent to 77.5 percent. As noted earlier, large increases in employment were experienced by CalWORKs participants. Similarly, employment among people living in poverty increased from 41.9 percent in 1993 to 45.6 percent in 1999.

---

[2]Hedderson and Schoeni (2001) proposed estimating employment by quarter, which was suggested in the LTFSS Countywide Evaluation Plan. However, quarterly estimates are not available by income and CalWORKs status; therefore, we provide annual estimates that are based on data that allow reporting by income and CalWORKs status.

Table 4.1 Nonheadline Indicators for Economic Well-Being in Los Angeles County: 1990–1999

Indicator	90	91	92	93	94	95	96	97	98	99
Percentage of adults 18-61 employed any time during the year	78.2	76.2	74.9	72.5	73.9	74.0	74.5	76.3	76.9	77.5
Percentage of income used for housing								23.0		20.7

Housing costs as a share of income typically decline when the economy expands, and this was the case in the late 1990s. Data are only available in 1997 and 1999, but in these two years, the share of income that is spent on housing declined from 23.0 percent to 20.7 percent. However, CalWORKs participants spend a much higher fraction of their income on housing: Among people on CalWORKs, the share of income spent on housing costs was 37 percent in 1997 and 31 percent in 1999. This high level of spending as a percentage of income is consistent with the notion that there are a minimum set of expenditures that are required to survive—housing, food, clothing—and even though expenditures on these items is lower for lower-income families, even the lowest-quality housing is expensive relative to income for these families. The most likely explanation for the rise and decline between 1997 and 1999 among CalWORKs participants is the increase in employment and earnings among welfare participants.

CONCLUSIONS

As shown above, the poverty rate has declined rapidly in Los Angeles County since the mid-1990s: 17 percent of Angelenos lived in families in which their income was below the poverty level in 1999, down from 25 percent in 1994; these trends are also seen in the rest of California and the nation as a whole. Despite the substantial improvements, the long-run trend over the 25 years for which data are available is for higher poverty. Of the potential explanations for this decline—the macroeconomy, demographics, and changes in poverty and welfare policy—the short-run fluctuations in poverty result primarily from changes in the macroeconomy and somewhat from changes in welfare policy; the long-run increase in poverty can be viewed in terms of demographics—the racial/ethnic composition of the population. Compared to 25 years ago, a higher percentage of Angelenos are Hispanics, a group with a high poverty rate. Eighteen of the 46 LTFSS Plan projects are expected to affect poverty, including two of the largest. Forecasts are difficult to predict, because they depend heavily on future economic conditions; however, forecasts range from a high of 18 percent to a low of 14 percent. While there is little that LTFSS programs can do to alter the macroeconomy, they may be able to dampen the effects of economic downturns. If not, the County may incur significant costs—from increased expenditures on social services to decreased tax revenues—when the poverty rate increases. Other indicators of economic well-being follow trends similar to those for poverty.

5. SOCIAL AND EMOTIONAL WELL-BEING: PERSONAL BEHAVIORS HARMFUL TO SELF OR OTHERS

Within the social and emotional well-being outcome area, the LTFSS Plan specified four indicators: (1) harmful behaviors to self or others, (2) access to quality child care, (3) participation in community activities, and (4) parent–child time together. Three indicators—access to quality child care; parent–child time together, and an index of harmful behavior to self and others that includes substance abuse and domestic violence—were placed on the Data Development Agenda and are therefore not discussed in this report. Harmful behaviors to self and others, child abuse and neglect, is the headline indicator. Child abuse and neglect is measured as the number of substantiated reports per 1,000 children. Substantiated reports include cases of physical abuse, sexual abuse or exploitation, emotional abuse, severe neglect, general neglect, and caretaker absence or incapacity. To be considered a substantiated case, the incident must first be reported to DCFS authorities, whereupon the report is initially assessed to decide if it falls within the definition of child abuse and neglect. If the report is accepted, it is then assigned to an emergency response investigator. During the investigation process, the DCFS worker must gather information about the alleged child abuse and neglect and then determine that the circumstances meet the agency's criteria for substantiation.

ESTABLISHING THE BASELINE

Figure 5.1 shows that child abuse and neglect declined in Los Angeles County during the 1990s, but the decline was not monotonic. Between 1990 and 1992, the rate fell from 32 to 23 reports per 1,000. However, this fall was followed by a substantial rise to 37 reports by 1996. After 1996, the rate declined in each of the subsequent four years, leaving the rate at 15 reports per 1,000, or one-half the level that existed at the beginning of the decade.

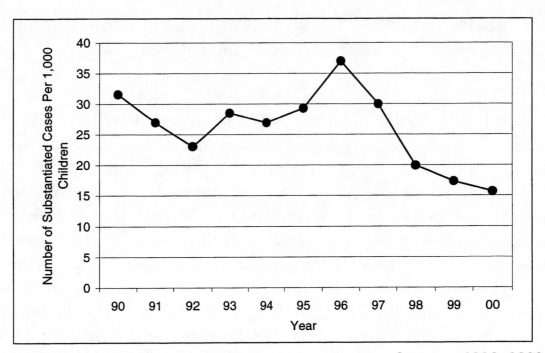

Figure 5.1—Child Abuse and Neglect in Los Angeles County: 1990–2000

When comparing the trends in the County with the trends in the rest of California and the nation (Figure 5.2), the rates were 80 percent higher in the County than they were in the rest of California and the rest of the nation at the beginning of the 1990s. However, by the end of the decade, these gaps were relatively small. Although the rates in the rest of the nation had improved in the last half of the 1990s, the improvements were much larger in Los Angeles County.

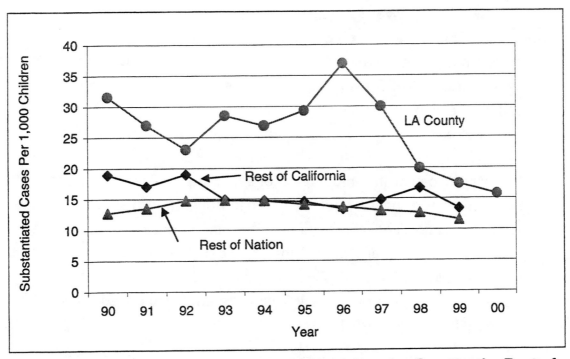

Figure 5.2—Child Abuse and Neglect in Los Angeles County, the Rest of California, and the Rest of the Nation: 1990–2000

THE STORY BEHIND THE BASELINE

The research literature suggests that the changes in child abuse and neglect in the 1990s were largely the result of two factors: (1) changes in the extent to which incidents of child abuse and neglect were translated into substantiated cases; and (2) changes in socioeconomic factors, including income, poverty, welfare use, and neighborhood characteristics. Each factor is discussed below.

Changes in the Reporting and Substantiation Process

It is important to note that the rate of child abuse and neglect, as measured by substantiated cases, is an underestimate of the true level of child abuse and neglect in the community. As with domestic violence discussed in Chapter 3, cases must be reported to authorities and then the case must be substantiated. Information from a national survey of professionals who work with children suggests that only 28 percent of the children the professionals identified as maltreated were ever investigated by child protective services (Sedlak and Broadhurst, 1996). Therefore, changes in reporting of abuse and substantiation of claims can have a significant effect on the trends in child abuse and neglect, as measured in the LTFSS evaluation. In other words, any fluctuation in this indicator may be caused by changes in the reporting and the substantiation process, as well as by the underlying incidence of child abuse and neglect.

One way to gauge the importance of reporting and substantiation is to examine emergency response referrals for child abuse and neglect. All cases reported to the authorities come through the emergency response referral system. These data are available from the DCFS. Figure 5.3 displays the trend in referrals during the 1990s in the County, which is generally consistent with the trend in substantiated cases of abuse.[1] That is, referrals increased from 1992 to 1996 and then declined through 1999.

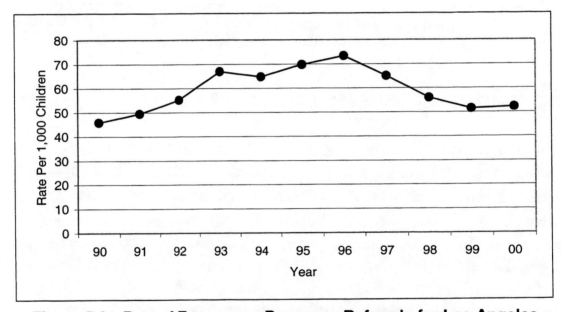

Figure 5.3—Rate of Emergency Response Referrals for Los Angeles County: 1990–2000

---

[1]The average number of children involved in each emergency response referral is roughly two in California. Therefore, to obtain a child-based count of the number of referrals, the number of referrals was multiplied by two. This number was then divided by the number of children in the County, in thousands, to express it as a rate per 1,000 children.

The large drop between 1997 and 1998 for both referrals (Figure 5.3) and substantiated cases (Figure 5.1) may also result from changes in reporting and filing systems. There was a major change in data collection procedures in the County that began in 1997 and was completed by May 1998. The DCFS changed from the older Child Information System to the statewide CWS-CMS automated system during this period. Sources within DCFS have speculated that some referrals and cases may have been inadvertently dropped during the initial period of adjustment to the new management information system. Unfortunately, we cannot gauge the extent to which this may have occurred. This is an important issue that needs to be resolved to better understand the baseline trend in substantiated cases of child abuse and neglect in Los Angeles County.

Type of Abuse and Neglect. Child abuse and neglect can take (at least) one of four forms: physical abuse, sexual abuse or exploitation, emotional abuse, or neglect. A recent study found that the national decline in abuse and neglect in the 1990s was largely the result of reductions in cases of *sexual* abuse (Jones and Finkelhor, 2001). Advocacy groups representing alleged perpetrators have lobbied state legislatures to toughen reporting and substantiation of sexual abuse claims to reduce the chances that parents will be wrongly accused. The authors suggest that efforts like these have created a possible "child abuse backlash," inhibiting both victims and professionals from reporting sexual abuse because of concerns about false allegations. However, the authors do not rule out the possibility that the decline represents a true increase in child safety because of the increased public awareness about child abuse in general and sexual abuse in particular.

Figures 5.4 and 5.5 display rates of child abuse and neglect by specific type of abuse for the County and the nation, respectively (U.S. Department of Health and Human Services, 2001). The changes in child abuse and neglect in the County largely result from changes in the rates of physical abuse and neglect (which includes severe neglect, general neglect, and caretaker absence or incapacity). Mimicking the overall trends in child abuse and neglect, physical abuse and neglect increased from 1992 to 1996 and then fell dramatically in

1997 and 1998. Substantiated sexual abuse and exploitation also follow a similar, but much weaker, pattern.

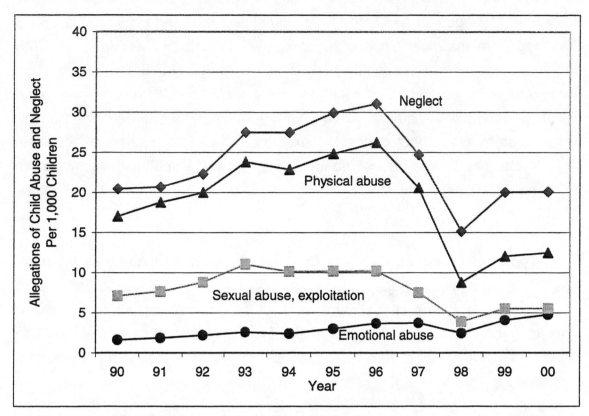

Figure 5.4—Child Abuse and Neglect Allegations in Los Angeles County, by Type of Abuse: 1990–2000

The pattern of abuse in the County is somewhat similar for the nation in the second half of the 1990s (Figure 5.5). Specifically, the improvements were greatest for physical abuse, neglect, and sexual abuse. Nationally, the rates of these types of cases declined by about 1 percentage point between 1995 and 1999, with more modest changes for other types of abuse. However, the changes in the nation between 1995 and 1999 were much smaller than the changes in the County, with physical abuse dropping from 24.8 to 12.0 in the County and from 3.6 to 2.5 in the nation (Figure 5.5).

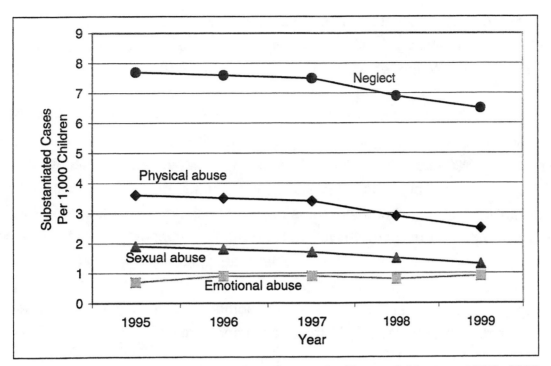

Figure 5.5—National Victimization Rates, by Type of Abuse: 1995–1999

Changes in Socioeconomic Factors

Evidence from both large-scale studies using state-level administrative data and smaller case studies suggest that child abuse and neglect is closely associated with economic factors, such as receipt of welfare, poverty, and income (Gelles, 1992; Gillham et al., 1998; Lee and George, 1999; Sedlak and Broadhurst, 1996; Waldfogel, 1998), as well as with other social problems such as domestic violence, mental illness, and substance abuse (Chaffin, Kelleher, and Hollenberg, 1996; Dore, 1993; Eckenrode et al., 2000; English, Marshall, and Orme, 1999; Wolock et al., 2001).

Paxson and Waldfogel (2001) demonstrate a strong negative association between neglect (and out-of-home care) and benefit levels. California was one of the states with declining monthly benefit levels during most of the 1990s. In 1992, a family of four would have received $1,178 per month in Aid to Families with Dependent Children (AFDC) plus Food Stamps; by 1997, that amount had decreased to $1,073.[2] At the same time, some evidence suggests that receipt of AFDC was associated with a higher risk of reports of abuse, but not substantiations (Wolock et al., 2001; Needell et al., 1999).

Several studies find that child abuse and neglect is associated with characteristics of the neighborhood (Drake and Pandey, 1996; Garbarino and Sherman, 1980; Zuravin, 1989). One of the most extensive recent studies examined child abuse in Cleveland and found dramatic differences in substantiated child maltreatment rates between neighborhoods (Coulton, Korbin, and Su, 1999). Both family-level variables (social support, income, violence, education, and marital status) and structural neighborhood factors (poverty and child care burden) were significant predictors of the child abuse potential score. However, family perceptions of the neighborhood process (perceived quality, facilities, disorder, and lack of control of children) were not.

In sum, the research has clearly shown a strong link between child abuse and family poverty or income, welfare benefit levels, and neighborhood characteristics. The implication for Los Angeles County is that the recession of the early to mid-1990s, which caused an increase in poverty and rise in welfare participation, was most likely an important cause of the increase in the child abuse and neglect rate, while the subsequent improvements in the labor market and poverty contributed to the decline in the late 1990s. Evidence of the close—but not perfect—connection can be seen in Figure 5.6.

---

[2]In 1998, the last year for which they present data on benefits levels, the amount rose to $1,136.

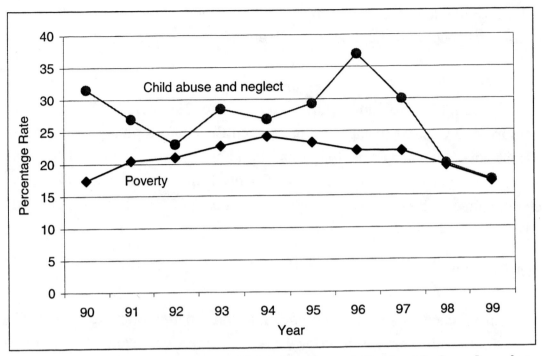

Figure 5.6—Poverty Rate and Child Abuse and Neglect in Los Angeles County: 1990–1999

Finally, there is a portion of the decline that cannot be explained by the factors described above. This, in combination with the unknown impact of the County database changes that were noted earlier, makes it impossible to fully explain the remainder of the decline. Although the decline in child abuse and neglect since 1996 is encouraging, it is yet unknown whether this has occurred because of an increase in child safety resulting from public awareness of prevention efforts, a change in parental behavior, community and environmental factors, earlier intervention, or a change in reporting.

PROJECTS TARGETING CHILD ABUSE AND NEGLECT

Eighteen projects list child abuse and neglect as an indicator that they expect to affect. Four of these projects have funding of at least $2 million over five years. Project 17—Community-Based Teen Services—is the largest LTFSS project, and it plans to leverage public schools, community-based organizations, County departments, other public agencies, and parents and teens themselves to integrate services to help teens avoid pregnancy, graduate from high school, read at grade level, and reject violence. Project 18—Teens with Special Needs—also targets teens, specifically teens who are underrepresented.

Project 26—Safe Places—will establish places of safety within communities for children and youths to go. Project 38—Multi-Disciplinary Family Inventory and Case Planning—will have each CalWORKs participant engage in a family inventory, where the families strengths and needs will be assessed, including the family's involvement with County Departments other than DPSS, including the Probation Department and DCFS. $7.0 million is allocated to Project 38.

FORECASTS

Three forecasts are reported based on three different sets of assumptions (Figure 5.7). The forecasts are developed to predict what would happen in the absence of the LTFSS Plan. The first forecast—the "medium" estimate—is based on the assumption that the economy will hold steady at its current level (i.e., the unemployment rate will not change). The second forecast—the "low" estimate—assumes that the long-run (linear) decline in child abuse and neglect during the 1990s will continue to occur through 2003. The third forecast—the "high" estimate—is based on the assumption that the key driving force behind changes in child abuse and neglect is the economy and that the economy will weaken in the coming years. Specifically, it assumes that the unemployment rate of 5.4 percent in 2000 will increase to 7.2 percent by 2003, which is the level that existed in the County around 1998. Moreover, because the relationship between the unemployment rate and child abuse and neglect is not well established in the research literature, we estimate this relationship (using regression analysis) for the County using the data on these two outcomes during the 1990 to 2000 period. Based on this historical relationship and the assumed increase in the unemployment rate, a "high" estimate is projected.

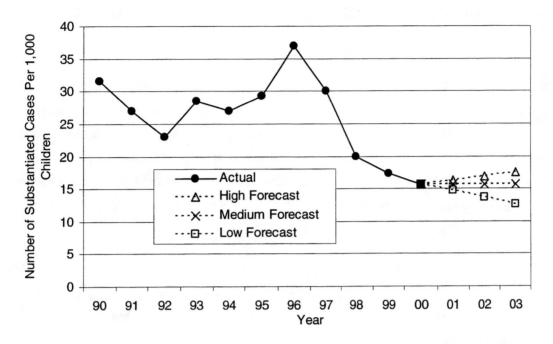

Figure 5.7—Forecast of Child Abuse and Neglect in Los Angeles County: 2001–2003

Through 2003, the three forecasts range from a high of 18 reports per 1,000 to a low of 13 reports per 1,000. In all three cases, the rate remains at a low level relative to much of the 1990s. However, given the large variation in child abuse and neglect in the past several years, accurately predicting its future path is difficult.

The baseline trend in substantiated cases of child abuse and neglect shows significant improvements starting in 1996. There remains, however, much room for further improvements. In the absence of the LTFSS Plan, the "high" forecast suggests that substantiated cases of child abuse and neglect may increase over the next two years. Such a result is costly for families and the community as a whole. In addition to the effects on social and emotional well-being, there are monetary costs associated with child abuse and neglect. These include medical and mental health care, foster care, and other social services. Consequently, reducing the incidence of child abuse and neglect both improves public safety and may reduce costs.

OTHER INDICATORS OF SOCIAL AND EMOTIONAL WELL-BEING

There are four other indicators in the social and emotional well-being outcome area, and three of them are on the Data Development Agenda. Thus, in addition to personal behavior harmful to self or others, participation in community activities is the only other indicator measured. The specific measure used for this report is the percentage of the voting-age population (18 and older) who voted in the most recent election. Countywide estimates for the 1996, 1998, and 2000 elections are reported in Table 5.1, with more-detailed estimates and data sources provided in Appendix B.

Table 5.1 Nonheadline Indicators for Social and Emotional Well-Being in Los Angeles County: 1990–2000

Indicator	90	91	92	93	94	95	96	97	98	99	00
Percentage of the voting-age population who voted in the November election							43.4		37.7		44.0
Percentage of the voting-age population who were registered to vote in the November election							50.1		47.7		49.5
Percentage of registered voters who voted in the November election							86.8		78.9		89.0

Voting is historically substantially higher in presidential election years (1996 and 2000). Therefore, it is most useful to compare changes in voting in 1996 with 2000. There was virtually no change between 1996 and 2000, with roughly 44 percent of age-eligible voters turning out to vote in Los Angeles County. These rates are much lower than they are for the rest of the nation, where in 2000, 65 percent of the voting age population voted.[3]

---

[3]The population age 18 and over is considered age-eligible to vote. This measure does not consider other eligibility factors, such as citizenship. Further, it does not reflect voter registration. When these factors are considered, voter turnout in the County is quite similar to estimates for the nation.

The lower turnout rates in the County can be completely explained by the racial/ethnic composition of the population. Within each racial/ethnic group, Angelenos were at least as likely to vote as were people outside the County. For example, although only 29 percent of Hispanics in the County voted in 2000, the same share of Hispanics outside of the County voted in that year. The large gap in age-eligible voting rates likely results from the fact that many Hispanics and Asians are not citizens and, thus, are not eligible to vote. As evidence, among registered voters, the percentage who voted was slightly higher in Los Angeles County than in the rest of the nation.

In sum, the social and emotional well-being outcome area has a limited set of information available to globally assess this area. The current measures—child abuse and voting behavior—do not effectively represent the broad area of social and emotional well-being that should be measured in the community. The Data Development Agenda should focus on this outcome area as one for substantial improvement.

CONCLUSIONS

As shown above, child abuse and neglect has declined in Los Angeles County during the 1990s, but the decline was not monotonic. After falling from 32 to 23 reports per 1,000 between 1990 and 1992, it rose to 37 reports in 1996 and then fell during each of next four years, ultimately reaching 15 reports in 1999. Of the potential explanations—changes in the extent to which incidents were translated into substantiated cases and changes in socioeconomic factors—both had some effect. In terms of the former, changes in reporting, changes in response of child safety officials, and/or a true change in the incidence of child abuse may be a factor, but it is not yet clear which of the three are reflected in the changes observed in the 1990s. As for the latter, research clearly shows a strong link between child abuse and family poverty or income, welfare benefit levels, and neighborhood characteristics. Eighteen of the LTFSS Plan projects are expected to affect poverty, including four with funding of at least $2 million over five years. High, low, and medium forecasts out to 2002 are projected to be 17.5, 15.7, and 12.6 reports per 1,000. Although there has been improvement in this area, there is much room for further improvement; if the high forecast materializes, the result could be costly for families and the community as a whole, including monetary costs for medical and mental health care, foster care, and other social services. In terms of other indicators of social well-being, almost all are on the Data Development Agenda, which means there is a limited set of information available to globally assess social and emotional well-being. Thus, the Data Development Agenda should focus on this outcome area for substantial improvement.

6. EDUCATION AND WORKFORCE READINESS: TEENAGE HIGH SCHOOL GRADUATION

Within the education and workforce readiness outcome area, the LTFSS Plan specified six indicators: (1) adult educational attainment, (2) elementary and secondary school students' reading at grade level, (3) teenage high school graduation, (4) mother's educational attainment at child's birth, (5) high school graduation for mothers who gave birth before high school graduation, and (6) adults enrolled in education or vocational training. The fifth of these six indicators was placed on the Data Development Agenda. Teen high school graduation was chosen as the headline indicator. This indicator is defined as the number of public high school graduates in a given year divided by the number of ninth-graders in public schools three years earlier.

ESTABLISHING THE BASELINE

Completing a high school degree has long-reaching implications both for future educational attainment and for success in the labor market. There are dramatic differences in earnings between high school graduates and those with less than a high school education. Similarly, having a college education leads to greater earnings than having a high school diploma. To attend a four-year college, one must first complete the requisite step of finishing high school (or community college training). In addition, given changes in the labor market over the past few decades that have awarded higher economic returns to those with higher levels of educational attainment, students who do not complete high school shut themselves off from higher lifetime earnings. In short, while a high school degree was sufficient for entry into a rewarding career two generations ago, it now provides insufficient preparation for employment in an economy that increasingly depends on technical skills.

The high school graduation rate was virtually unchanged in Los Angeles County during the period for which estimates are available, 1997–2000, as shown in Figure 6.1. The estimates imply that 62 percent of ninth-graders graduate from high school within four years. This rate is lower than the rate in the rest of California, where 71 percent of ninth-graders in the 1996–97 academic year graduated in 2000; however, the rate in California follows a similar flat trend, as it does in the United States as a whole.

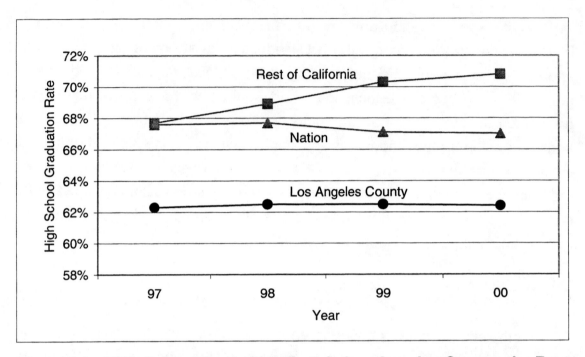

Figure 6.1—High School Graduation Rate in Los Angeles County, the Rest of California, and the Nation as a Whole: 1997–2000

This indicator draws on the best available data. However, the measure suffers from important limitations. Most important, the measure assumes that there is no movement of students in or out of the County during the high school years, or that at least the movements in and out are perfectly offsetting. For example, consider the case where all ninth-graders graduate on time, implying a true high school graduation rate of 100 percent. However, if a large number of students enrolled in ninth grade in the County moved out of the County before they graduated—and much fewer students moved in—then the rate of high school graduation as measured here would be less than 100 percent. Or if a large number of ninth-graders in public schools transferred to private schools before graduation—and a smaller number of private-school ninth-graders transferred to public schools—then the high school graduation rate would again be less than 100 percent. In general, in a dynamic county like Los Angeles, assuming that a population is not growing and is immobile is a tenuous assumption at best.   This said, data limitations prevent more-accurate assessments of this outcome for a sufficient number of years in the 1990s.

THE STORY BEHIND THE BASELINE

The research suggests that the factors affecting high school completion include demographics, family background, labor market forces, and public policy. Each is discussed below.

Demographics

While the overall trend for high school graduation rates has been fairly flat, stark differences exist in high school graduation rates by student race/ethnicity. In 2000, the teenage high school completion rate overall in the County was 62.4 percent. However, broken down by race/ethnicity, the rate ranges from a low of 52.4 percent for Hispanic students to a high of 90.1 percent for Asian students; the graduation rate for Black, non-Hispanic students was 56.8 percent, and it was 77.4 percent for non-Hispanic Whites.   National data on high school dropouts suggests that among Hispanic students, those born outside the 50 states and the District of Columbia had a *dropout* rate of 44.2 percent, compared to a dropout rate of about 16 percent for first- and second-generation Hispanic students.   Hence, the relatively low high school *graduation* rate for Hispanic students overall is driven by a relatively high dropout rate for Hispanic students who are recent immigrants (U.S. Department of Education, 2000).   Given the sizable population of recent Hispanic immigrants in the County, the low high school graduation rate for this group likely has an impact on the Countywide rate.

Family Background

The family background characteristics that research has found to be associated with high school completion are parents' educational attainment, family income, region of the country where the student lives, and community residence (e.g., urban/rural/suburban).

Parents' educational attainment is positively correlated with the likelihood that a student will graduate from high school. The correlation is particularly strong when the parents have a college degree (Eide and Showalter, 2001; Eide and Ronan, 2001).

Students who live in wealthier families are more likely to complete high school, and those in poorer families are less likely to complete high school. Data from the U.S. Department of Education show that young people who live in families in the lowest 20 percent of the income distribution were five times more likely to drop out of high school than youth who live in families in the top 20 percent of the income distribution (U.S. Department of Education, 2000, Table 1).

The type of community in which a student resides is related to the high school graduation rate. In general, research suggests that students who live in an urban area are less likely to graduate from high school than are comparable students who live in suburban communities (Eide and Showalter, 2001). Moreover, the relation between urbanicity and high school completion is found to differ somewhat by race, with the correlation being statistically stronger for Black men than for White men, White women, or Black women.

Labor Market Forces

The strength of the labor market can also influence the high school graduation rate. When the unemployment rate is low and the wages for low-skill jobs are relatively high, then the "opportunity cost" of high school attendance and getting a degree increases. In other words, such circumstances would entice students who are at the point of indifference between staying in school and dropping out ("on the margin") to drop out of school and enter the labor market. In their minds, staying in school has become too expensive, and so they opt for entry into the labor market. The converse is also true when the employment and wage opportunities for teenagers are more dire; more students would choose to stay in school, all else equal.

Public Policy

A school or district could adopt a variety of policies that may influence the high school graduation rate, either intentionally or unintentionally. A few of the more common policies, which are discussed below, are implementation of grade retention (or its flipside of social promotion), changes in "school quality" measures, and participation in extracurricular activities.

Grade retention generally refers to the practice of having a child who did not meet performance standards repeat a grade in school to bring academic performance to the requisite level. Grade retention is widely practiced throughout the nation. For 1995, the National Center for Education Statistics (NCES) estimated that over 13 percent of individuals age 16 to 24 had repeated at least one grade. For Blacks, the estimate is nearly 1 in 5[0] (National Center for Education Statistics, 97-473, Table 24, 1997).

Proponents of grade retention argue that they are taking a "get tough" stance on student achievement, while opponents of grade retention claim that it is correlated with negative outcomes, such as dropping out of high school. For example, it has been estimated that retaining a student increases the probability that the student will not complete high school by 20–30 percent (Grissom and Shepard, 1989). While it is not clear that repeating a grade *leads* to dropping out of high school as retention opponents claim, these two events do seem to be statistically significantly correlated.

Large, urban school districts throughout the United States, including the Los Angeles Unified School District, have done away with social promotion policies and have begun retaining students in much higher numbers. The correlation between grade retention and drop out may help to explain why the teenage high school graduation rate is somewhat lower in the County than it is in the rest of the nation.

Changes in "school quality," as measured by lowering class size, lengthening the school year, or increasing the percentage of teachers with an advanced degree, may help improve high school completion rates. In principle, improving the inputs into the education process should translate into improvements in the outputs from this process, such as educational attainment and student achievement. For example, lowering the class size would allow the teacher to spend more time with each student and maintain more control in the classroom, and hiring more teachers with higher levels of training should also result in better student outcomes if these teachers are indeed better prepared and more effective. The research literature on the relation between school quality variables and student outcomes is mixed (e.g., Hanushek, 1996; Card and Krueger, 1996); nevertheless, these are policies that are actively pursued by schools and districts and that are perceived by practitioners to be important policy variables.

Another way in which many administrators and policymakers believe that high school completion rates can be improved is to increase student participation in extracurricular activities. The fraction of students who participate in extracurricular activities is huge, with Department of Education data suggesting that over 80 percent of high school seniors participate in a school-sponsored extracurricular activity (U.S. Department of Education, 2000). Engaging in sports, music, drama, and other clubs and organizations is thought to increase a student's connection to the school and classmates and, hence, provide a richer educational experience that would translate into higher educational attainment. Many researchers believe that participation in extracurricular activities also builds self-confidence, self-discipline, and teamwork skills, which translate into a potentially improved educational experience. Of course, a related policy consideration is that with the majority of students participating in school-sponsored activities, a sizable portion of the school budget will be allocated to these largely non-academic ventures, hence reducing the amount that can be spent on other areas that are directly related to student learning. Moreover, the more time students spend on extracurricular activities, the less time they spend studying.

PROJECTS TARGETING TEEN HIGH SCHOOL GRADUATION

Of all headline indicators, teen high school graduation is the target of the largest set of projects. In total, 22 projects expect to affect this indicator. Among these 22 projects, Community-Based Teen Services—Project 17—has the largest funding at $17.5 million over five years. Project 17 plans to leverage public schools, community-based organizations, County departments, other public agencies, and parents and teens themselves to integrate services to help teens avoid pregnancy, graduate from high school, read at grade level, and reject violence. Youth Jobs—Project 23—and Multi-Disciplinary Family Inventory—Project 38—are the two next largest projects. Youth Jobs is the successor to the Job Training Partnership Act (JTPA) Summer Youth programs, which will provide paid work-based learning opportunities for thousands of CalWORKs youths. The job experience is linked with functional basic skills enhancement, career planning, employment, employment readiness skills development, and job placement. The Multi-Disciplinary Family Inventory seeks to identify and address the human services needs, beyond traditional welfare-to-work activities, among CalWORKs participants.

FORECASTS

We present only a single (medium) forecast of the high school graduation rate (Figure 6.2). The teenage high school graduation rate was virtually unchanged over the four-year time period (1997–2000) for which data are available. Therefore, in the absence of the LTFSS Plan, we expect it to remain virtually unchanged. As noted earlier, labor market earnings are highly related to educational attainment. People without a high school diploma or General Education Degree (GED) are typically limited to low-wage jobs and are, thus, more vulnerable to economic downturns. This leads to greater hardship for the individual and potentially greater costs for the community. Because of the limited job market available to people who have not completed a high school degree, they are more likely to need social services, such as housing assistance or job training programs. In addition, low-wage jobs often do not provide fringe benefits, such as health insurance, and, thus, public hospitals and clinics may be the primary source of health care for these workers and their families. Without improvements in the teenage high school graduation rate, these costs are expected to remain relatively constant as well.

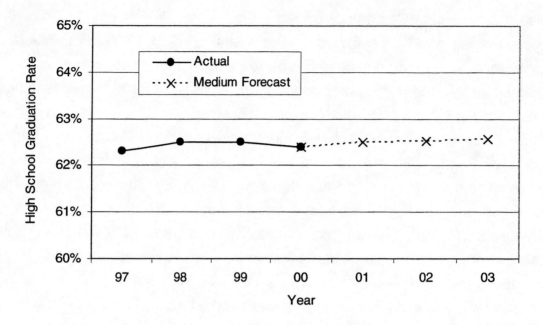

Figure 6.2—Forecast of High School Graduation Rate in Los Angeles County: 2001–2003

OTHER INDICATORS OF EDUCATION AND WORKFORCE READINESS

Of the six indicators in the education and workforce readiness outcome area, just one was placed on the Data Development Agenda. As opposed to the headline indicator, three of the four remaining indicators show favorable trends. Table 6.1 reports the Countywide estimates of these non-headline indicators, with more detailed estimates and data sources reported in Appendix B. Adult educational attainment, as measured by the percentage of adults 18 to 45 who have completed a high school degree or GED, has increased gradually during the 1990s, from 70.2 percent in 1990 to 73.8 percent in 2000. Although we only have three years of data on how third-graders are performing in the California Standardized Testing and Reporting program, we are seeing improvements. The educational attainment of mothers giving birth increased by almost one full year, from 11.0 in 1991 to 11.7 in 1999. These improvements were experienced among all racial/ethnic groups, in all Supervisorial Districts (SDs), and in almost all eight Service Planning Areas (SPAs) (Appendix Table B.17).

Table 6.1 Nonheadline Indicators for Education and Workforce Readiness in Los Angeles County: 1990–2000

Indicator	90	91	92	93	94	95	96	97	98	99	00
Percentage of people 18–45 who have completed a high school degree or GED	70.2	72.2	73.4	72.9	72.9	72.1	72.9	72.0	72.1	73.7	73.8
Percentage of 3rd graders performing at or above median for grade in the California Standardized Testing and Reporting program									29.0	31.0	34.0
Average years of education among women giving birth		11.0	11.0	11.1	11.1	11.2	11.3	11.5	11.6	11.7	
Percentage of people 18–45 who are enrolled in education or vocational training		17.0	15.3	15.9	16.3	14.4	18.3	18.2	17.7	17.7	

CONCLUSIONS

As shown above, the teenage high school graduation rate in Los Angeles County was virtually unchanged over the past four years, with 62 percent of ninth-graders graduating within four years. This rate is lower than the rate in the rest of California (71 percent) and in the nation as a whole, although both the California and national trends follow the same flat trajectory. Of the potential explanations for this trend—demographics, family background, labor market forces, and public policy—demographics plays a substantial role. While the overall trend is flat, stark differences occur by student race/ethnicity, with Hispanics having the lowest rate of high school graduation. This rate is, in turn, driven by the even higher dropout rates of recent Hispanic immigrants. Given the sizable population of recent Hispanic immigrants in the County, the low high school graduation rate for this group likely has an impact on the Countywide rate. Of all the headline indicators, this one is the target of the largest set of LTFSS Plan projects—22 out of the 46. As for forecasts, we believe the rate is not likely to deviate from the recent historical patterns; thus, our medium forecast is 62.6 percent out to 2003, with the high and low forecasts projected to be no more than 10 percent different from our medium forecast. Without improvements in this indicator, the costs associated with it are likely to remain relatively constant as well. As for the other indicators of education and workforce readiness, three of the four show favorable trends.

7. CONCLUSIONS AND NEXT STEPS

CONCLUSIONS

As shown by the assessment in the preceding five chapters, the baseline trends in the majority of the headline indicators show general improvements during the 1990s. Domestic violence arrests have increased from 1988 to 1998, which we view as an improvement in community safety reflecting changes in police behavior, given that the evidence indicates, at the national level, that there is no increase in victimization or actual incidents of domestic violence. The percentage of people living in families whose income is below the federal poverty threshold has been declining rapidly since the mid-1990s, with Angelenos living in poverty dropping from 25 percent in 1994 to 17 percent in 1999. Finally, child abuse and neglect also declined during the 1990s, falling from 32 cases per 1,000 children in 1990 to 15 cases in 1999, or one-half the level that existed at the beginning of the decade.

The percentage of low weight births and teenage high school graduation rates are the exceptions. The low birth weight rate increased in the County, the rest of California, and the nation as a whole during the 1990s, which is a departure from improvements in low birth weight rates that were made nationally during the 1960s and 1970s. The teenage high school graduation rate has not declined, but it has not increased either, remaining relatively constant across the years for which we have data.

Similarly, the forecasts for the headline indicators imply that the County could incur considerable costs, monetary and societal, if it does not intervene and sustain efforts to improve the trends forecasted for the indicators and, by extension, the outcome areas. Together, the projects making up the LTFSS Plan and other preventive efforts are intended to improve outcomes and thus avoid these substantial costs associated with low birth weight infants, not having a high school diploma (or GED), domestic violence, child abuse, and families living in poverty. These baseline data presented in this report should help the County determine whether the current allocation of resources among the projects will target the outcomes that it deems of highest priority.

NEXT STEPS

This report provides the County with the baseline trends. The ultimate goal—but not the subject of this document—is to update the trendlines for the indicators as the LTFSS Plan is implemented and then compare these trendlines for the period before and after the LTFSS Plan has been implemented to determine net impacts. The updating will occur in each year of the three-year contract between RAND and Los Angeles County. Baseline outcome data will be compared to post-Plan outcomes when those data become available. The LTFSS Plan will most likely be fully implemented by the end of 2002, which suggests that data are needed for at least 2002 and 2003 before post-Plan outcomes can be measured. In addition, delays in the release of data sources range from six months to two years, implying that estimates for 2002 and 2003 will be available no sooner than 2004 and, in many cases, not until 2005.

In the meantime, the measurement of the indicators will proceed along three dimensions. First, as more recent data become available in the future, these data will be analyzed and the indicators measured, with the estimates added to the current charts. Second, measurement of the indicators for additional subgroups will be explored. Third, the items on the Data Development Agenda will be addressed.

APPENDIX A. INITIAL FUNDING FOR EACH PROJECT AND THE HEADLINE INDICATORS THE PROJECTS EXPECT TO AFFECT

Table A.1 lists the 46 projects that are funded by the LTFSS Plan, the headline indicators they target, and the amount of initial funding that each has been allocated.

Table A.1 List of Projects, Initial Project Funding, and Headline Indicators the Projects Are Expected to Affect

Project Number and Name	Low Birth Weight	Domestic Violence Arrests	Annual Income Under Poverty	Child Abuse/ Neglect	Teenage HS Graduation	Initial LTFSS Plan Funding, 5 Years ($m)
1. CalWORKs WtW Strategy			X			$4.00
2. Employer-Linked Education/Training			X			$2.50
3. Transitional Subsidized Employment			X			$0.00
4. County Apprenticeship Program			X			$0.00
5. Business Micro-Loan and Incubator			X			$1.00
6. Housing Relocation Program						$7.80
7. Strategic Info — Supp Job Creation			X			$0.33
8. Community Economic Development			X			$0.50
9. Mini-Career Centers			X			$1.50
10. Community Outreach -- Health Care	X					$5.00
11. Hotline to Resolve Health Care						$0.00
12. Health Care Transportation						$0.00
13. Health First						$0.00
14. Transitional Support--Homeless						$9.48
15. Emergency Assistance--Eviction						$0.00
16. Housing Counseling/Training						$0.50
17. Community-Based Teen Services				X	X	$17.50
18. Teens with Special Needs				X	X	$2.50
19. Emancipated Foster Youth-Parents				X	X	$0.55
20. Teen Passport to Success				X	X	$0.74
21. Staff Dev for Teen Svc Providers				X	X	$0.50
22. Cal-Learn and Teen Parents					X	$2.40
23. Youth Jobs					X	$6.75
24. Public Library Services for					X	$0.68

Children						
25. Operation READ					X	$0.79
26. Safe Places				X	X	$2.40
27. DART/STOP for CW Families		X		X		$0.00
28. Domestic Violence Prevention		X		X		$0.65
29. School-Based Probation Supervision					X	$2.10
30. Support -- Fam of Probation Child					X	$0.15
31. Strategic Support for Child Care						$5.00
32. Federal Family Supp Svcs Network						$4.50
33. LTFSS Family Preservation						$8.50
34. Home Visitation Program	X					$5.25
35. Peer Self-Help Support Groups	X	X	X	X	X	$0.28
36. Support and Therapeutic Options						$0.60
37. School Attendance Areas	X	X	X	X	X	$0.10
38. Multi-Disciplinary Family Inventory	X	X	X	X	X	$7.00
39. County Family Resource Centers	X	X	X	X	X	$1.35
40. Strategic Planning Data Centers	X	X	X	X	X	$0.58
41. SPA Council Staff and Tech Asst.	X	X	X	X	X	$0.64
42. CalWORKs Systems Review	X	X	X	X	X	$0.50
43. New Directions L-T Fam Comm	X	X	X	X	X	$0.00
44. CalWORKs Case Management	X	X	X	X	X	$0.00
45. TranStar Enhancement						$0.22
46. L-T Family Self-Suff Evaluation	X	X	X	X	X	$2.00
Total Number of Projects Expecting to Impact Headline Indicators	12	12	18	18	22	

APPENDIX B. DATA SOURCES AND ESTIMATES OF ALL INDICATORS NOT ON THE DATA DEVELOPMENT AGENDA

This appendix includes two sets of tables. The first set—B.1–B.18—provides the estimates for each of the 18 indicators not on the Data Development Agenda, with one table devoted to each indicator. Estimates are reported for the period 1990–2000, when available. Estimates for earlier years are not reported even when they are available because of space constraints. The evaluation requires measuring the indicators for various subgroups (e.g., CalWORKS participants, people in poverty, etc.), and estimates for each of these groups, when available, are also contained in these tables.

Estimates are reported for Supervisorial Districts (SDs) and Service Planning Areas (SPAs) for some indicators. In some cases the individual data that was used to construct these estimates were only reported at the zip code or census-tract level. Therefore, a crosswalk, which was developed by the Los Angeles County Department of Health Services (Los Angeles County DHS), was used to map the zip code and census-tract data into SDs and SPAs.

A list of the definitions and data sources used to measure each indicator is provided in the second set of tables—B.19 and B.20. A detailed discussion of the sources is provided in Hedderson and Schoeni (2001). A careful selection of data sources is essential to accurately estimating each indicator. The data sources are of two types: surveys and administrative files. Scores of surveys have been conducted of Los Angeles County that contain some information pertinent to the proposed indicators. Similarly, scores of administrative files contain information pertinent to the proposed indicators. Nevertheless, there are relatively few data sources that have covered the County using a consistent measure for a long period of time at a low level of geography.

The March Current Population Survey, CPS, which is used to measure several indicators, does not ask about income for individuals under 15. Therefore, we assume that a child under 15 is on CalWORKs if anyone in the household is receiving CalWORKs.

The precision of the estimates vary across indicators. For example, the estimates of low birth weight, mother's educational attainment at child's birth, and infant mortality are based on birth certificates of every child born in the County in each year. Therefore, these estimates are precise. However, some estimates are based on survey data in which the sample sizes are small, which reduces the precision of the estimates. *Therefore, one should be extremely careful when interpreting the estimates reported in Tables B.1–B.18. Not all differences are significant in a statistical sense.* Space is not available to provide estimates of the precision of each and every estimate.

Table B.1 Infant Mortality

Operational Definition: Number of babies born alive each year who die within 12 months of birth per 1,000 live births in that year.

	1990	1991	1992	1993	1994	1995	1996	1997	1998	1999	2000
Los Angeles County											
Countywide	8.0	7.7	7.4	7.2	7.0	6.7	5.9	5.9			
Race/Ethnicity											
Hispanic	7.2	6.9	6.9	6.3	6.2	6.0	5.4	5.7			
White, non-Hispanic	6.8	6.6	5.9	5.9	5.8	5.5	5.0	4.4			
Black, non-Hispanic	16.0	16.4	15.2	15.9	16.3	14.4	12.8	12.2			
Asian, non-Hispanic	5.7	5.8	5.2	6.3	4.8	5.1	4.9	4.5			
Supervisory Districts											
SD-1	7.2	7.4	6.6	6.4	6.1	6.3	5.9	5.9			
SD-2	10.0	9.6	9.7	9.3	9.1	7.6	7.5	7.4			
SD-3	6.6	6.9	6.2	6.1	6.3	6.0	4.8	5.5			
SD-4	7.9	6.8	6.8	7.2	6.7	7.0	5.2	5.3			
SD-5	7.0	6.9	6.7	6.3	6.0	6.1	5.6	5.2			
Service Planning Areas											
Antelope Valley (1)	9.6	9.9	8.7	8.2	8.8	7.5	5.6	9.0			
San Fernando Valley (2)	6.7	6.5	6.5	5.9	6.3	5.8	4.9	4.8			
San Gabriel Valley (3)	7.6	7.0	6.3	6.4	5.7	6.4	5.9	5.6			
Metro (4)	6.6	8.0	6.6	6.1	6.9	6.3	5.4	5.8			
West (5)	6.0	6.7	7.4	5.9	5.4	5.6	4.5	4.0			
South (6)	11.2	10.8	10.9	10.2	9.6	8.2	8.2	8.3			
East (7)	6.6	6.6	7.0	6.9	6.3	6.2	5.9	5.8			
South Bay (8)	8.8	7.2	6.6	8.0	7.4	7.5	6.0	5.8			
Rest of California											
All	7.9	7.3	6.8	6.7	6.9	6.2	5.8	6.0			
Race/Ethnicity											
Hispanic	7.4	7.2	6.1	6.3	6.5	6.0	5.6	5.6			
White, non-Hispanic	7.2	6.6	6.2	6.1	6.5	5.6	5.3	5.5			
Black, non-Hispanic	16.0	14.6	15.9	14.4	14.2	12.8	12.0	13.9			
Asian, non-Hispanic	6.8	5.7	5.9	5.3	5.9	5.0	4.8	4.8			
Rest of USA											
All	9.2	8.9	8.5	8.4	8.0	7.6	7.3	7.2	7.2		
Race											
White	7.6	7.3	6.9	6.8	6.6	6.3	6.1	6.0			
Black	18.0	17.6	16.8	16.5	15.8	15.1	14.7	14.2			

Table B.2 Low Birth Weight Births

Operational Definition: Number of babies born alive each year who weigh less than 2,500 grams per 1,000 live births per year.

	1990	1991	1992	1993	1994	1995	1996	1997	1998	1999	2000
Los Angeles County											
Countywide	6.1	6.1	6.1	6.2	6.4	6.4	6.4	6.5	6.6	6.6	6.4
Race/Ethnicity											
Hispanic	5.1	5.1	5.3	5.4	5.5	5.6	5.5	5.7	5.7	5.7	5.6
White, non-Hispanic	5.2	5.3	5.4	5.6	5.8	6.1	6.2	6.0	6.3	6.3	6.8
Black, non-Hispanic	13.0	13.0	12.9	12.5	13.0	12.7	12.3	12.3	12.2	12.5	12.0
Asian, non-Hispanic	5.6	6.1	6.0	5.9	6.4	6.4	6.8	6.9	7.1	6.8	6.7
Supervisory Districts											
SD-1	5.4	5.2	5.5	5.7	6.0	6.0	5.8	6.0	6.1	5.9	6.1
SD-2	7.5	7.5	7.3	7.2	7.3	7.3	7.3	7.4	7.5	7.3	7.2
SD-3	5.6	5.5	6.0	5.7	6.0	6.1	6.0	6.1	6.5	6.3	6.0
SD-4	5.6	5.6	5.6	5.8	5.9	6.1	6.3	6.3	6.2	6.5	6.1
SD-5	5.3	5.5	5.6	5.8	6.1	6.3	6.1	6.4	6.5	6.6	6.5
Service Planning Areas											
Antelope Valley (1)	5.2	5.4	5.6	6.0	7.0	7.2	6.3	7.2	6.8	7.8	7.2
San Fernando Valley (2)	5.4	5.3	5.7	5.6	5.8	5.9	5.7	6.0	6.3	6.2	5.9
San Gabriel Valley (3)	5.6	5.5	5.7	6.0	6.0	6.1	6.1	6.2	6.3	6.1	6.3
Metro (4)	5.8	5.8	6.2	6.0	6.3	6.7	6.3	6.3	6.8	6.4	6.3
West (5)	5.4	5.7	6.3	5.9	6.7	6.0	6.4	6.6	6.9	6.7	6.8
South (6)	8.1	8.0	7.9	7.6	7.6	7.7	7.8	7.8	7.9	7.9	7.5
East (7)	4.9	5.0	5.0	5.3	5.7	5.5	5.7	5.8	5.6	5.9	5.7
South Bay (8)	6.4	6.4	6.0	6.3	6.4	6.8	6.7	6.7	6.5	6.8	6.7
Rest of California											
All	5.7	5.7	5.8	5.9	6.1	5.9	5.9	6.0	6.1	5.9	6.1
Race/Ethnicity											
Hispanic	5.3	5.3	5.3	5.5	5.5	5.4	5.4	5.5	5.5	5.4	5.6
White, non-Hispanic	5.0	5.0	5.1	5.2	5.5	5.4	5.4	5.4	5.6	5.4	5.6
Black, non-Hispanic	12.2	12.5	12.6	12.9	12.3	11.7	11.7	12.0	11.4	11.4	11.5
Asian, non-Hispanic	6.2	6.4	6.4	6.1	6.5	6.4	6.7	6.8	6.9	6.9	7.1
USA											
All	7.0	7.1	7.1	7.2	7.3	7.3	7.4	7.5	7.6	7.6	
Race/Ethnicity											
Hispanic	6.1	6.1	6.1	6.2	6.2	6.3	6.3	6.4	6.4	6.4	
White, non-Hispanic	5.6	5.7	5.7	5.9	6.1	6.2	6.4	6.5	6.6	6.6	
Black, non-Hispanic	13.3	13.6	13.4	13.4	13.3	13.2	13.1	13.1	13.2	13.2	
Asian											

- 83 -

Table B.3 Birth to Teens

Operational Definition: Number of live births to girls 10–17 per 1,000 girls 10–17. For the USA, the estimates are reported for girls 15–17 years old.

	1990	1991	1992	1993	1994	1995	1996	1997	1998	1999	2000
Los Angeles County											
Countywide		20.7	20.0	19.6	19.3	18.7	16.9	15.2	13.8	12.5	
Race/Ethnicity											
Hispanic		30.0	29.8	29.2	28.8	28.3	25.7	23.5	20.9	19.2	
White, non-Hispanic		7.8	6.5	6.1	5.8	5.5	4.6	3.6	3.4	2.8	
Black, non-Hispanic		26.4	24.7	23.8	23.2	20.9	18.4	15.9	14.7	12.4	
Asian, non-Hispanic		3.4	2.9	3.0	3.1	2.9	2.6	2.6	2.5	2.2	
Supervisory Districts											
SD-1		23.6	23.5	22.7	22.2	21.6	19.7	18.3	17.1	15.1	
SD-2		29.0	27.4	26.7	25.3	24.3	21.0	19.1	17.3	16.2	
SD-3		15.1	14.9	13.8	13.4	13.0	12.5	11.3	10.6	9.4	
SD-4		16.9	14.8	14.9	14.8	14.1	13.1	12.2	10.9	9.9	
SD-5		10.2	10.1	9.4	10.0	9.4	8.7	7.8	7.1	6.9	
Service Planning Areas											
Antelope Valley (1)		16.5	14.1	14.2	16.0	15.4	14.0	13.5	12.9	12.2	
San Fernando Valley (2)		13.5	13.3	12.2	12.3	11.6	11.3	10.3	9.2	8.7	
San Gabriel Valley (3)		14.8	15.0	14.6	14.8	14.6	12.8	11.6	10.8	9.9	
Metro (4)		23.7	24.0	21.9	20.8	20.7	17.6	17.0	16.4	14.0	
West (5)		8.0	7.5	6.3	5.9	6.5	6.0	5.0	4.3	4.2	
South (6)		36.3	34.4	33.2	31.4	29.0	25.8	23.4	21.3	20.6	
East (7)		20.3	19.1	19.2	19.2	18.2	17.4	16.0	14.6	12.9	
South Bay (8)		18.6	16.2	16.7	15.8	15.5	14.0	12.5	11.1	9.8	
Rest of California											
All		16.1	16.0	16.0	15.8	15.1	13.8	12.9	11.8	10.8	
Hispanic		29.7	30.2	31.0	31.6	30.5	28.8	27.1	24.8	23.3	
White, non-Hispanic		8.6	8.2	7.9	7.5	7.0	6.0	5.4	5.0	4.2	
Black, non-Hispanic		29.5	28.6	27.2	24.8	24.8	21.0	19.5	16.2	14.4	
Asian, non-Hispanic		9.2	8.9	8.5	8.6	8.0	7.1	6.5	5.7	5.1	
USA											
All	37.5	38.7	37.8	37.8	37.6	36.0	33.8	32.1	30.4	28.7	
Hispanic	65.9	70.6	71.4	71.7	74.0	72.9	69.0	66.3	62.3	61.3	
White, non-Hispanic	23.2	23.6	22.7	22.7	22.8	22.0	20.6	19.4	18.4	17.1	
Black, non-Hispanic	84.9	86.7	83.9	82.5	78.6	72.1	66.6	62.6	58.8	53.7	
Asian	16.0	16.1	15.2	16.0	16.1	15.4	14.9	14.3	13.8	12.3	

Table B.4 Individuals without Health Insurance

Operational Definition: Percentage of people without health insurance.

	1990	1991	1992	1993	1994	1995	1996	1997	1998	1999	2000
Los Angeles County											
Countywide	26.2	26.2	26.9	26.1	29.1	28.9	27.5	29.1	30.1	28.7	23.1
CalWORKs/TANF/AFDC Status											
Not Enrolled	27.6	27.8	28.8	28.2	31.8	31.0	29.3	30.9	31.1	29.9	24.0
Enrolled	2.0	2.2	2.5	4.1	2.1	5.4	2.4	3.0	4.2	5.0	2.7
Below Poverty Level	46.5	46.9	43.2	44.3	43.6	40.0	40.6	39.7	48.1	45.6	38.0
Race/Ethnicity											
Hispanic	42.6	41.6	42.8	37.1	40.8	39.9	38.4	43.1	43.4	41.1	35.9
White, non-Hispanic	13.7	13.7	13.5	14.0	15.2	16.7	14.3	12.2	13.9	13.7	10.0
Black, non-Hispanic	16.5	18.1	18.1	22.5	21.7	25.2	20.5	17.5	19.0	21.0	13.7
Asian, non-Hispanic	22.1	22.4	23.6	25.4	35.6	25.5	30.4	30.8	34.3	31.2	22.0
Rest of California											
All	16.1	15.4	16.0	17.1	17.8	17.0	17.0	18.3	18.9	17.1	16.0
CalWORKs/TANF/AFDC Status											
Not Enrolled	17.0	16.4	16.9	18.2	19.0	18.0	17.9	19.1	19.6	17.7	16.6
Enrolled	2.1	1.1	2.6	1.2	1.0	2.1	1.9	2.8	2.4	1.6	0.3
Below Poverty Level	31.7	29.7	31.8	33.8	32.4	32.4	31.1	32.8	33.0	34.7	32.7
Race/Ethnicity											
Hispanic	32.0	28.5	30.0	27.5	30.3	32.0	29.0	30.6	34.7	29.2	29.5
White, non-Hispanic	11.2	11.0	11.4	12.6	12.7	11.5	11.5	13.1	12.6	11.1	9.9
Black, non-Hispanic	16.8	15.8	15.2	17.4	17.6	16.6	21.5	17.3	21.7	20.8	13.2
Asian, non-Hispanic	15.7	15.2	15.1	17.7	16.4	14.7	19.4	19.7	15.9	17.4	14.1
Rest of USA											
All	13.5	13.6	14.3	14.9	14.6	14.8	15.2	15.7	15.8	15.1	13.7
CalWORKs/TANF/AFDC Status											
Not Enrolled	14.1	14.3	14.9	15.6	15.3	15.5	15.7	16.1	16.2	15.4	13.9
Enrolled	2.0	1.6	2.1	1.9	2.0	1.5	2.2	1.9	2.2	2.1	1.2
Below Poverty Level	27.8	27.6	27.6	28.3	28.2	29.6	30.4	31.2	31.8	31.8	
Race/Ethnicity											
Hispanic	30.5	29.5	30.5	30.5	32.4	32.1	32.8	32.7	34.1	32.2	31.4
White, non-Hispanic	10.7	10.7	11.4	11.9	11.5	11.4	11.5	12.0	11.8	11.0	9.7
Black, non-Hispanic	19.8	20.7	20.1	20.3	19.5	20.7	21.6	21.2	22.0	21.0	18.3
Asian, non-Hispanic	16.1	17.5	19.1	19.6	18.1	19.5	19.9	19.4	19.0	19.7	17.2

Table B.5 Domestic Violence Arrests

Operational Definition: Arrests for domestic violence per 100,000 population per year.

	1990	1991	1992	1993	1994	1995	1996	1997	1998	1999	2000
Los Angeles County											
Countywide	251.2	250.3	261.3	249.5	266.3	274.4	271.6	276.7	252.1	229.2	211.7
Rest of California											
All	176.0	184.1	199.4	211.3	239.4	254.5	250.2	265.1	230.0	206.5	203.6
Rest of USA											
All											

Table B.6 Child Placement in Out-of-Home Care

Operational Definition: Children placed in out-of-home care during the year per 1,000 persons under the age of 18. Out-of-home care refers to living outside of the home of the parent or related caretaker.

	1990	1991	1992	1993	1994	1995	1996	1997	1998	1999	2000
Los Angeles County											
Countywide	4.6	4.4	4.4	4.8	4.5	4.5	5.2	4.7	3.4	3.2	
Rest of California											
All	3.2	2.9	2.8	2.8	3.1	3.0	3.1	3.5	3.9	3.6	

Table B.7 Youth Arrests for Violent Crimes

Operational Definition: Youth arrests per 100,000 youths per year for homicide, forcible rape, robbery, aggravated assault, or kidnapping. Youths are persons under the age of 18. These arrests do not necessarily result in complaint filings and convictions; these events happen after the arrests, and data on them are not available.

	1990	1991	1992	1993	1994	1995	1996	1997	1998	1999	2000
Los Angeles County Countywide	1064.8	949.2	913.0	817.9	773.0	772.8	724.3	646.5	590.8	535.6	
Rest of California All	479.6	533.6	544.4	560.4	594.4	565.2	544.0	518.4	500.4	476.4	
Rest of USA All											

Table B.8 Homicide Rate

Operational Definition: Number of homicides per 100,000 persons in that year.

	1990	1991	1992	1993	1994	1995	1996	1997	1998	1999	2000
Los Angeles County											
Countywide	21.4	22.5	22.8	22.0	19.4	18.8	15.8	13.4	10.6	9.5	
Race/Ethnicity											
Hispanic	19.3	19.6	18.3	19.7	16.7	13.4	11.7	9.8	7.4	6.7	
White, non-Hispanic	8.5	8.4	8.3	8.1	6.8	6.8	6.2	5.5	4.6	3.3	
Black, non-Hispanic	92.4	97.4	109.1	95.6	88.8	94.6	76.1	65.3	51.8	47.9	
Asian, non-Hispanic	6.6	11.7	8.1	9.2	6.4	7.9	6.5	4.1	3.7	4.2	
Supervisory Districts											
SD-1	22.5	22.1	24.9	21.4	21.7	23.3	16.1	15.0	11.6	10.3	
SD-2	46.8	47.0	50.5	49.0	44.3	37.9	34.6	25.9	20.8	19.4	
SD-3	11.9	13.1	11.9	12.3	8.8	9.9	7.1	8.0	6.2	5.2	
SD-4	13.8	15.6	14.6	14.7	12.4	13.0	12.1	10.9	9.4	7.6	
SD-5	6.3	9.3	8.7	9.9	7.2	8.2	8.1	5.7	4.5	4.4	
Service Planning Areas											
Antelope Valley (1)	6.2	11.2	12.4	9.8	12.5	11.8	11.8	8.5	7.3	5.2	
San Fernando Valley (2)	8.7	12.1	10.4	10.4	7.0	8.3	7.1	6.7	5.6	5.2	
San Gabriel Valley (3)	11.3	11.9	13.4	13.7	12.1	13.2	9.4	8.4	6.6	6.5	
Metro (4)	26.6	26.6	30.6	25.7	21.1	24.4	18.0	16.0	9.9	9.5	
West (5)	9.3	9.3	9.7	11.7	9.0	7.3	8.8	5.4	4.9	3.3	
South (6)	69.0	66.7	72.3	72.5	65.3	55.1	49.5	36.1	29.2	30.0	
East (7)	15.6	19.3	16.4	14.4	16.1	17.6	14.5	12.8	11.5	8.6	
South Bay (8)	19.6	19.6	19.6	20.2	17.8	15.7	14.3	13.7	11.6	8.6	
Rest of California*											
All	12.4	13.4	13.4	13.6	12.3	11.3	9.4	8.6	7.2		
Rest of USA*											
All	9.9	10.4	9.9	9.9	9.4	8.6	7.8	7.3	6.6		

* Source=CDC WONDER.

Table B.9 Adults Employed

Operational Definition: Percentage of adults 18–61 who were employed at any time during the year.

	1990	1991	1992	1993	1994	1995	1996	1997	1998	1999	2000
Los Angeles County											
Countywide	78.2	76.2	74.9	72.5	73.9	74.0	74.5	76.3	76.9	77.5	79.2
CalWORKs/TANF/AFDC Status											
Not Enrolled	79.8	78.9	77.1	75.4	76.8	76.8	76.6	78.1	77.8	78.7	80.1
Enrolled	27.8	11.9	20.7	21.1	23.0	20.4	22.6	24.6	36.7	32.5	43.0
Below Poverty Level	48.1	43.0	43.7	41.9	40.1	43.2	43.5	42.5	47.2	45.6	44.5
Race/Ethnicity											
Hispanic	73.5	71.2	69.4	68.6	68.8	70.9	73.6	71.3	73.3	74.8	75.4
White, non-Hispanic	83.0	81.4	80.2	79.3	80.6	80.8	79.9	84.3	83.4	82.1	85.2
Black, non-Hispanic	76.1	71.3	68.6	66.5	74.3	66.4	68.2	72.4	75.4	74.2	79.7
Asian, non-Hispanic	77.9	78.3	77.9	68.6	69.6	70.4	67.9	74.4	72.5	75.6	74.4
Rest of California											
All	81.1	80.6	79.5	79.3	80.5	79.6	80.2	80.7	80.3	80.6	81.3
CalWORKs/TANF/AFDC Status											
Not Enrolled	83.0	82.6	81.7	81.3	82.5	81.6	81.9	81.7	81.1	81.1	81.9
Enrolled	34.3	30.7	31.7	34.3	35.5	31.8	32.3	47.6	49.0	58.6	50.7
Below Poverty Level	47.0	50.0	47.0	48.2	45.1	45.7	47.5	50.1	46.2	49.9	51.6
Race/Ethnicity											
Hispanic	77.1	74.8	75.5	73.8	74.8	75.3	77.2	78.0	77.8	77.7	77.0
White, non-Hispanic	83.8	83.6	81.6	83.4	84.3	83.2	82.3	82.7	83.6	83.9	84.3
Black, non-Hispanic	72.7	74.9	73.1	70.0	78.6	63.4	74.6	76.2	67.3	76.1	77.7
Asian, non-Hispanic	74.8	75.3	77.8	73.0	72.5	79.2	78.0	79.1	76.3	73.8	79.2
Rest of USA											
All	82.6	82.2	81.8	81.4	82.2	82.2	82.6	82.7	82.6	83.1	82.8
CalWORKs/TANF/AFDC Status											
Not Enrolled	84.1	83.9	83.4	83.1	83.6	83.4	83.7	83.5	83.2	83.5	83.2
Enrolled	36.2	34.5	35.4	36.1	37.3	39.3	41.5	46.8	50.3	54.8	48.4
Below Poverty Level	49.4	49.3	48.7	48.2	48.9	48.8	49.0	49.5	49.3	51.1	49.0
Race/Ethnicity											
Hispanic	74.9	75.1	74.1	73.4	73.7	73.6	75.2	76.0	76.1	77.4	78.0
White, non-Hispanic	85.0	84.6	84.3	84.1	84.9	85.0	85.2	85.0	84.9	85.1	84.8
Black, non-Hispanic	73.7	73.4	72.5	72.3	73.4	73.4	74.7	76.1	76.4	78.2	77.4
Asian, non-Hispanic	75.6	74.7	76.1	74.1	75.6	76.7	79.2	79.3	78.5	77.0	78.4

Table B.10 Annual Income under Poverty Level

Operational Definition: Percentage of people living in families with income under the federal poverty threshold.

	1990	1991	1992	1993	1994	1995	1996	1997	1998	1999	2000
Los Angeles County											
Countywide	17.4	20.5	21.0	22.8	24.2	23.3	22.0	21.9	19.6	17.1	15.8
CalWORKs/TANF/AFDC Status											
Not Enrolled	14.8	16.7	17.1	18.7	19.1	19.3	18.5	18.1	17.7	14.8	13.5
Enrolled	64.7	76.7	72.6	65.9	76.1	68.0	71.5	78.9	68.1	63.3	65.9
Race/Ethnicity											
Hispanic	28.7	33.0	33.7	35.4	34.9	34.8	31.5	32.3	30.1	25.6	22.0
White, non-Hispanic	7.1	8.9	9.8	9.1	10.9	9.6	11.2	9.2	6.6	7.4	7.9
Black, non-Hispanic	25.6	27.5	25.3	22.3	28.3	26.8	22.7	30.1	20.9	19.7	17.3
Asian, non-Hispanic	8.7	11.6	11.4	18.5	19.9	16.9	18.4	12.2	16.3	10.7	15.3
Rest of California											
All	12.4	13.6	13.5	16.3	15.2	13.9	14.8	14.4	13.7	12.5	11.8
CalWORKs/TANF/AFDC Status											
Not Enrolled	9.3	9.6	9.8	12.8	12.0	10.7	11.2	11.5	11.2	10.9	10.2
Enrolled	58.5	71.2	66.1	65.3	62.9	60.5	76.4	73.1	69.0	56.6	54.0
Race/Ethnicity											
Hispanic	23.9	25.5	23.5	28.6	27.4	24.8	27.8	23.1	22.8	22.3	21.0
White, non-Hispanic	7.6	8.7	9.4	9.7	9.2	7.1	8.9	9.7	9.8	8.3	7.1
Black, non-Hispanic	23.9	19.9	24.2	33.7	19.1	27.6	20.9	21.1	20.0	19.4	13.8
Asian, non-Hispanic	15.2	17.2	12.0	15.8	17.3	17.5	16.2	16.3	10.2	9.0	10.8
Rest of USA											
All	13.4	14.0	14.3	14.9	14.2	13.5	13.4	12.9	12.5	11.6	11.1
CalWORKs/TANF/AFDC Status											
Not Enrolled	10.1	10.5	10.9	11.4	11.2	10.7	10.9	10.8	10.7	10.3	10.1
Enrolled	75.5	77.5	75.8	76.1	73.1	70.6	72.3	75.3	73.5	67.7	65.7
Race/Ethnicity											
Hispanic	27.9	27.9	28.4	29.8	29.9	29.4	29.0	26.2	24.9	22.3	21.1
White, non-Hispanic	8.9	9.4	9.6	9.9	9.4	8.5	8.6	8.6	8.2	7.7	7.5
Black, non-Hispanic	32.0	32.9	33.5	33.2	30.6	29.1	28.3	26.2	26.0	23.7	22.1
Asian, non-Hispanic	12.8	14.2	12.6	14.7	13.9	14.3	13.7	14.0	11.6	10.4	10.3

Table B.11 Percentage of Family Income Used for Housing

Operational Definition: Among all people, the ratio of average family spending on housing to average family income, multiplied by 100.

	1990	1991	1992	1993	1994	1995	1996	1997	1998	1999	2000
Los Angeles County											
Countywide		21.9		24.3		24.1		22.9		20.8	
CalWORKs/TANF/AFDC Status											
Not Enrolled		21.4		23.7		23.3		22.2		20.3	
Enrolled		29.1		34.2		36.1		36.0		30.1	
Below Poverty Level		73.2		79.3		62.8		68.3		71.4	
Race/Ethnicity											
Hispanic		24.6		28.9		27.7		26.4		23.4	
White, non-Hispanic		19.5		21.5		21.4		19.5		18.4	
Black, non-Hispanic		19.6		26.5		22.8		25.3		22.2	
Asian, non-Hispanic		24.6		24.4		25.0		23.9		22.1	
Rest of California											
All		21.1		22.0		22.7		20.7		20.2	
CalWORKs/TANF/AFDC Status											
Not Enrolled		21.0		21.9		22.3		20.3		20.7	
Enrolled		24.2		24.0		37.6		34.2			
Below Poverty Level		76.2		81.4		74.9		68.8		78.3	
Race/Ethnicity											
Hispanic		24.5		25.6		30.3		23.6		19.7	
White, non-Hispanic		20.5		20.8		21.2		19.4		19.8	
Black, non-Hispanic		24.3		24.7		24.9		22.8		22.4	
Asian, non-Hispanic		20.0		23.6		22.3		21.5		21.5	
Rest of USA											
All		17.2		17.5		18.1		17.5		16.6	
CalWORKs/TANF/AFDC Status											
Not Enrolled		16.9		17.3		17.8		17.2		16.4	
Enrolled		26.8		26.5		27.7		27.3		22.7	
Below Poverty Level		48.9		54.2		59.1		63.6		62.9	
Race/Ethnicity											
Hispanic		20.9		21.8		21.9		21.3		19.7	
White, non-Hispanic		16.7		16.9		17.3		16.7		15.7	
Black, non-Hispanic		19.4		20.2		20.4		20.2		20.2	
Asian, non-Hispanic		20.0		20.2		20.5		20.5		19.3	

Table B.12 Personal Behavior Harmful to Self or Others

Operational Definition: Substantiated cases of children abused or neglected per 1,000 children per year.

	1990	1991	1992	1993	1994	1995	1996	1997	1998	1999	2000
Los Angeles County											
Countywide	31.6	27.0	23.0	28.5	26.9	29.3	37.0	30.0	19.9	17.3	15.7
Rest of California											
All	18.9	17.0	19.0	14.8	14.7	14.5	13.3	14.8	16.7	13.4	
Rest of USA											
All	12.7	13.5	14.7	14.8	14.7	14.1	13.7	13.0	12.7	11.5	

Table B.13 Participation in Community Activities

Operational Definition: (1) Percentage of registered voters that voted in the November election; (2) Percentage of voting age population that were registered to vote in the November election; (3) Percentage of voting age population that voted in the November election.

	Percentage of registered voters that voted in the November election			Percentage of the voting-age population that were registered to vote in the November election			Percentage of the voting-age population that voted in the November election		
	1996	1998	2000	1996	1998	2000	1996	1998	2000
Los Angeles County									
Countywide	86.8	78.9	89.0	50.1	47.7	49.5	43.4	37.7	44.0
Race/Ethnicity									
Hispanic	83.1	78.7	88.9	23.6	23.3	29.2	19.6	18.3	25.9
White, non-Hispanic	88.5	80.6	90.0	72.1	69.4	67.1	63.8	55.9	60.4
Black, non-Hispanic	85.3	82.6	87.6	72.8	71.9	66.6	62.1	59.4	58.4
Asian, non-Hispanic	83.4	63.6	85.0	36.1	33.6	38.9	30.1	21.4	33.1
Rest of California									
All	86.2	77.3	87.7	59.2	54.5	54.6	51.1	42.1	47.9
Race/Ethnicity									
Hispanic	76.2	75.3	79.1	32.9	31.3	29.7	25.0	23.6	23.5
White, non-Hispanic	88.0	79.8	90.0	72.1	66.8	67.6	63.4	53.3	60.8
Black, non-Hispanic	85.1	56.3	80.6	61.8	54.1	58.7	52.5	30.5	47.3
Asian, non-Hispanic	83.3	71.0	83.5	30.7	30.8	31.0	25.5	21.9	25.9
Rest of USA									
All	82.1	67.2	85.5	62.6	62.6	64.5	54.6	42.1	55.1
Race/Ethnicity									
Hispanic	74.2	57.5	77.4	35.3	35.3	35.8	27.9	20.3	27.7
White, non-Hispanic	83.1	68.2	86.3	67.9	67.9	70.0	59.5	46.3	60.4
Black, non-Hispanic	79.6	65.1	84.0	60.6	60.6	64.2	50.6	39.4	53.9
Asian, non-Hispanic	78.8	66.2	82.6	28.4	28.5	29.4	25.3	18.9	24.3

Table B.14 Adult Attainment of a High School Diploma or GED

Operational Definition: Percentage of people 18 to 45 who have completed high school or a General Education Degree.

	1990	1991	1992	1993	1994	1995	1996	1997	1998	1999	2000
Los Angeles County											
Countywide	70.2	72.2	73.4	72.9	72.9	72.1	72.9	72.0	72.1	73.7	73.8
CalWORKs/TANF/AFDC Status											
Not Enrolled	70.6	72.8	74.3	74.0	74.2	73.2	74.2	73.3	72.8	74.2	74.6
Enrolled	58.4	52.0	49.0	43.4	44.3	50.4	45.9	38.0	49.9	46.1	40.5
Below Poverty Level	46.1	43.2	44.6	43.7	45.9	48.3	43.9	49.2	48.4	47.3	52.1
Race/Ethnicity											
Hispanic	41.3	44.9	45.5	42.4	46.4	46.5	47.9	43.0	46.2	48.7	48.3
White, non-Hispanic	87.3	87.9	91.2	91.4	90.2	90.5	91.7	92.5	92.2	91.4	92.8
Black, non-Hispanic	81.8	79.6	82.1	80.1	85.4	86.5	81.6	85.6	88.6	88.8	90.2
Asian, non-Hispanic	90.1	87.0	84.8	89.2	87.7	83.9	85.3	86.3	85.0	88.5	84.7
Rest of California											
All	79.1	79.0	80.1	81.0	80.9	80.7	81.0	82.6	82.5	82.2	82.4
CalWORKs/TANF/AFDC Status											
Not Enrolled	79.9	80.0	81.0	81.6	81.9	81.7	81.8	83.4	83.1	82.8	82.8
Enrolled	51.8	49.5	53.5	64.8	56.0	54.4	55.2	57.3	56.0	54.5	57.4
Below Poverty Level	51.2	54.0	56.1	61.2	59.9	54.7	51.0	56.7	62.0	64.5	60.1
Race/Ethnicity											
Hispanic	48.5	45.8	48.3	51.7	51.6	50.5	51.2	55.3	54.3	54.3	55.1
White, non-Hispanic	86.9	88.0	88.9	88.8	90.6	90.8	90.5	90.8	91.6	91.3	91.3
Black, non-Hispanic	80.9	79.8	81.8	85.4	83.6	91.5	83.9	86.6	84.8	86.8	85.8
Asian, non-Hispanic	72.9	76.9	79.0	85.3	85.6	80.8	82.0	85.3	82.9	82.3	87.3
Rest of USA											
All	77.8	78.6	79.4	80.3	80.8	81.4	81.4	81.8	82.5	82.9	83.4
CalWORKs/TANF/AFDC Status											
Not Enrolled	78.5	79.3	80.2	80.9	81.5	82.0	81.9	82.3	82.9	83.2	83.7
Enrolled	51.9	52.7	54.3	58.2	60.0	60.7	60.3	60.3	59.5	61.6	57.6
Below Poverty Level	50.0	52.1	53.1	55.9	57.1	57.3	56.9	58.1	59.0	61.3	61.3
Race/Ethnicity											
Hispanic	53.4	53.1	54.7	55.4	55.5	54.8	55.2	56.7	57.3	57.8	58.2
White, non-Hispanic	81.4	82.4	83.2	83.9	84.6	85.4	85.4	85.7	86.5	86.9	87.6
Black, non-Hispanic	66.5	67.2	67.7	70.5	72.6	73.1	73.7	74.5	75.6	76.3	77.3
Asian, non-Hispanic	79.0	80.6	83.0	83.4	84.8	83.6	83.5	84.7	85.6	84.5	85.5

Table B.15 Elementary and Secondary School Students Reading at Grade Level

Operational Definition: Percentage of elementary and secondary students (third and ninth grade) performing at or above median for grade in the California Standardized Testing and Reporting program.

Third Grade Level	1990	1991	1992	1993	1994	1995	1996	1997	1998	1999	2000
Los Angeles County											
Countywide									29.0	31.0	34.0
Race/Ethnicity											
Hispanic									15.0	17.0	21.0
White, non-Hispanic									59.0	63.0	67.0
Black, non-Hispanic									22.0	26.0	30.0
Asian, non-Hispanic									53.0	57.0	62.0
Rest of California											
All									41.0	45.0	48.0
Race/Ethnicity											
Hispanic									18.0	22.0	26.0
White, non-Hispanic									59.0	64.0	68.0
Black, non-Hispanic									25.0	31.0	35.0
Asian, non-Hispanic									45.0	50.0	54.0

Ninth Grade Level	1990	1991	1992	1993	1994	1995	1996	1997	1998	1999	2000
Los Angeles County											
Countywide									26.0	26.0	27.0
Race/Ethnicity											
Hispanic									13.0	14.0	15.0
White, non-Hispanic									52.0	51.0	53.0
Black, non-Hispanic									17.0	19.0	19.0
Asian, non-Hispanic									48.0	48.0	51.0
Rest of California											
All									37.0	37.0	38.0
Race/Ethnicity											
Hispanic									16.0	16.0	17.0
White, non-Hispanic									53.0	53.0	54.0
Black, non-Hispanic									20.0	21.0	21.0
Asian, non-Hispanic									40.0	41.0	43.0

Table B.16 Teenage High School Graduation

Operational Definition: Ratio of the number of high school graduates to the number of students entering ninth grade three academic years previous.

	1990	1991	1992	1993	1994	1995	1996	1997	1998	1999	2000
Los Angeles County											
Countywide								62.3	62.5	62.5	62.4
Race/Ethnicity											
Hispanic								52.5	53.1	53.1	52.4
White, non-Hispanic								74.5	73.9	76.7	77.4
Black, non-Hispanic								56.0	54.6	54.0	56.8
Asian, non-Hispanic								90.3	92.7	89.9	90.1
Rest of California											
All								67.7	68.9	70.3	70.8
Race/Ethnicity											
Hispanic								55.5	56.7	58.9	59.7
White, non-Hispanic								73.6	75.0	76.7	77.6
Black, non-Hispanic								55.0	56.4	58.4	58.5
Asian, non-Hispanic								85.2	86.9	84.1	83.9
USA											
All								67.6	67.7	67.1	67.0

Table B.17 Mother's Educational Attainment at Child's Birth

Operational Definition: Average years of education among women giving birth in each year.

	1990	1991	1992	1993	1994	1995	1996	1997	1998	1999	2000
Los Angeles County											
Countywide		11.0	11.0	11.1	11.1	11.2	11.3	11.5	11.6	11.7	
Race/Ethnicity											
Hispanic		9.2	9.3	9.5	9.6	9.7	9.8	10.0	10.2	10.3	
White, non-Hispanic		13.7	13.8	13.9	13.9	14.0	14.0	14.2	14.2	14.4	
Black, non-Hispanic		12.6	12.6	12.6	12.6	12.6	12.7	12.8	12.8	12.9	
Asian, non-Hispanic		13.4	13.4	13.5	13.5	13.6	13.8	13.9	14.0	14.1	
Supervisory Districts											
SD-1		9.8	9.8	9.9	10.0	10.1	10.2	10.3	10.4	10.6	
SD-2		10.1	10.1	10.1	10.2	10.3	10.4	10.6	10.7	10.8	
SD-3		11.3	11.4	11.5	11.5	11.6	11.6	11.9	12.0	12.1	
SD-4		11.9	11.9	11.9	12.0	12.0	12.1	12.3	12.4	12.4	
SD-5		12.7	12.7	12.7	12.8	12.8	12.8	13.0	13.0	13.1	
Service Planning Areas											
Antelope Valley (1)		12.2	12.2	12.2	12.2	12.1	12.0	12.0	12.0	12.1	
San Fernando Valley (2)		11.6	11.6	11.7	11.8	11.8	11.9	12.0	12.1	12.2	
San Gabriel Valley (3)		11.5	11.5	11.6	11.6	11.7	11.7	11.9	12.0	12.1	
Metro (4)		9.8	9.8	9.9	10.0	10.2	10.2	10.4	10.5	10.8	
West (5)		13.7	13.6	13.6	13.6	13.8	13.8	14.0	14.2	14.3	
South (6)		9.5	9.5	9.6	9.6	9.7	9.8	9.9	10.0	10.1	
East (7)		10.6	10.7	10.8	10.8	10.9	10.9	11.1	11.2	11.3	
South Bay (8)		11.5	11.6	11.6	11.7	11.7	11.8	12.0	12.1	12.1	
Rest of California											
All		11.8	11.8	11.9	11.8	12.0	12.1	12.2	12.3	12.3	
Race/Ethnicity											
Hispanic		9.7	9.7	9.8	9.9	10.1	10.1	10.3	10.4	10.5	
White, non-Hispanic		13.3	13.4	13.5	13.5	13.6	13.7	13.7	13.8	13.9	
Black, non-Hispanic		12.4	12.5	12.5	12.4	12.5	12.6	12.6	12.7	12.7	
Asian, non-Hispanic		11.8	12	12.4	12.4	12.6	13	13.3	13.6	13.7	

Table B.18 Adult Participation in Education or Vocational Training
Operational Definition: Percent of people 18–45 who are enrolled in education or vocational training.

	1990	1991	1992	1993	1994	1995	1996	1997	1998	1999	2000
Los Angeles County											
Countywide		17.0	15.3	15.9	16.3	14.4	18.3	18.2	17.7	17.7	
Race/Ethnicity											
Hispanic		13.3	11.4	11.9	13.0	12.0	15.0	13.7	14.7	13.6	
White, non-Hispanic		17.5	15.9	17.3	17.9	14.9	19.7	19.6	20.5	18.5	
Black, non-Hispanic		21.0	17.7	18.2	16.0	21.6	19.1	23.4	19.6	19.8	
Asian, non-Hispanic		27.7	27.6	23.1	24.8	20.2	25.7	26.6	20.2	30.0	
Rest of California											
All		18.2	16.5	16.7	16.5	16.8	18.2	19.7	18.5	17.8	
Race/Ethnicity											
Hispanic		12.1	12.6	13.5	13.7	11.4	11.6	12.5	12.7	11.7	
White, non-Hispanic		19.1	16.6	16.6	17.0	18.2	19.9	20.7	19.2	18.9	
Black, non-Hispanic		16.9	16.2	23.1	18.4	19.4	22.9	26.0	20.8	17.9	
Asian, non-Hispanic		27.1	25.8	23.4	21.1	22.6	21.5	25.1	25.8	25.3	
Rest of USA											
All		15.8	15.9	16.0	16.1	16.0	16.0	16.1	16.4	15.8	
Race/Ethnicity											
Hispanic		12.2	13.2	13.9	13.7	13.3	12.7	12.4	12.9	12.4	
White, non-Hispanic		15.9	16.0	16.0	16.1	16.2	16.0	16.3	16.4	15.9	
Black, non-Hispanic		14.9	15.0	15.5	15.8	15.8	16.4	15.8	17.2	16.4	
Asian, non-Hispanic		26.5	24.9	25.6	25.6	24.4	23.3	23.5	23.9	22.6	

Table B.19 Definition of Indicators

Indicator	Conceptual Definition	Operational Definitions	
		Numerator	Denominator
1 Infant mortality	Deaths among infants	Number of infants who die within 12 months of birth	Number of live births (in 1000s)
2 Low weight births	Infants born weighing less than 2500 grams (5.5 lbs)	Number of infants born weighing less than 2500 grams (5.5 lbs)	Number of live births
3 Births to teens	Births to women age 10-17 years	Number of births to women age 10-17 years	Population of women age 10-17 years (in 1000s)
4 Individuals without health insurance	Individuals without health insurance	Number of people without health insurance	Population
5 Domestic violence arrests	Arrests for physical violence and intimidation between spouses and cohabitants	Number of arrests for domestic violence	Population 18 and older (in 100,000s)
6 Child placement in out-of-home care	Removal of children from their parents' or related caretakers' homes and temporary or permanent placement in another living situation	Number of children placed in out-of-home care	Population under age 18 (in 1000s)
7 Youth arrests for violent crimes	Violent crimes committed by persons under age 18	Number of arrests of people under age 18 for violent crimes	Population under age 18 (in 100,000s)
8 Homicide rate	Homicides committed	Number of homicide deaths	Population (in 100,000s)
9 Adults employed by quarter	Adults working for wages, salary, or profit	Number of people age 18-61 years who are employed	Population age 18-61 years
10 Annual income under poverty level	People living in poverty	Number of people living in families with income under the federal poverty threshold	Population
11 Percentage of family income used for housing	Amount of family housing costs relative to family income	Average ratio of housing spending to family income	Not applicable
12 Personal behavior harmful to self or others: child abuse	Prevalence of child abuse	Number of substantiated cases of child abuse and neglect	Population under age 18 (in 1000s)
13 Participation in community activities	Extent to which the population is engaged in activities within their communities	1. Number of people who voted 2. Number of people registered to vote 3. Number of registered voters who voted	1. Population age 18 and older 2. Population age 18 and older 3. Number of registered voters
14 Adult education; attainment of high school diploma, GED, or 8th grade reading level	Adults who attained basic education, knowledge, or skills in adulthood	Number of people 18 and older who have completed high school or received GED	Population age 18 and older
15 Elementary and secondardy school students reading at grade level	Elementary and secondardy school students reading at grade level	Number of 3rd (9th) grade students scoring greater than or equal to 50 percent of National Percentile Ranking on STAR exam	Number of 3rd (9th) grade students taking the test
16 Teenage high school graduation	Percentage of students entering high school who graduated within 4 years	Number of high school graduates in academic year X	Number of people enrolled in 9th grade in academic year X-3
17 Mother's educational attainment at child's birth	Educational attainment of new mothers	Average years of education among new mothers	Not applicable
18 Adult participation in education or vocational training	Adults enhancing their human capital by participating in education or vocational training	Number of people age 18-45 years enrolled in education or vocational training	Population age 18-45 years

Note: All indicators are measured at the annual level for all available years.

- 100 -

Table B.20 Data Sources

Indicator	Geo*	Description	Data Sources for Estimates Value**	Data Sources for Estimates Numerator	Data Sources for Estimates Denominator
1 Infant mortality	LA	Tabulations based on micro data files	Not applicable	California Birth Cohort File, CA Department of Health Services, Office of Health Information and Research	California Birth Cohort File, CA Department of Health Services, Office of Health Information and Research
	CA	Tabulations based on micro data files	Not applicable	California Birth Cohort File, CA Department of Health Services, Office of Health Information and Research	California Birth Cohort File, CA Department of Health Services, Office of Health Information and Research
	US	Published tabulations	For 1990-1993: Centers for Disease Control and Prevention, NCHS, Vital Statistics of the United States, vol. 11, Mortality part A For 1994-1997: Public Health Service, Final Data for 1997 National Vital Statistics Reports, vol. 48	Not applicable	Not applicable
2 Low weight births	LA	Tabulations based on micro data files	Not applicable	California Birth Statistical Master File, CA Department of Health Services, Office of Health Information and Research	California Birth Statistical Master File, CA Department of Health Services, Office of Health Information and Research
	CA	Tabulations based on micro data files	Not applicable	California Birth Statistical Master File, CA Department of Health Services, Office of Health Information and Research	California Birth Statistical Master File, CA Department of Health Services, Office of Health Information and Research
	US	Published tabulations	Not applicable	Not applicable	Not applicable
3 Births to teens	LA	Tabulations based on micro data files	Not applicable	California Birth Statistical Master File, CA Department of Health Services, Office of Health Information and Research	Walter R. MacDonald & Associates
	CA	Tabulations based on micro data files	Not applicable	California Birth Statistical Master File, CA Department of Health Services, Office of Health Information and Research	Walter R. MacDonald & Associates
	US	Published tabulations	Not applicable	Not applicable	Not applicable
4 Individuals without health insurance	LA	Tabulations based on micro data files	Not applicable	Current Population Survey, March Supplement	Current Population Survey, March Supplement
	CA	Tabulations based on micro data files	Not applicable	Current Population Survey, March Supplement	Current Population Survey, March Supplement
	US	Tabulations based on micro data files	Not applicable	Current Population Survey, March Supplement	Current Population Survey, March Supplement
5 Domestic violence arrests	LA	Tabulations	Not applicable	Report on Arrests for Domestic Violence in California, 1998; Criminal Justice Statistics Center, CA Department of Justice	Race/Ethnic Population with Age and Sex Detail, 1970-2040. State of California, Department of Finance, December 1998. http://www.dof.ca.gov/html/demograp/data.htm
	CA	Tabulations	Not applicable	Report on Arrests for Domestic Violence in California, 1998; Criminal Justice Statistics Center, CA Department of Justice	Race/Ethnic Population with Age and Sex Detail, 1970-2040. State of California, Department of Finance, December 1998. http://www.dof.ca.gov/html/demograp/data.htm
	US	Data not available	Not applicable	Not applicable	Not applicable
6 Child placement in out-of-home care	LA	Published tabulations	Needell, B., et al. (2001). Performance Indicators for Child Welfare Services in California: First Entries to Foster Care 1988-1999; First Entries, Child Population, and Incidence Rates	Not applicable	Not applicable
	CA	Published tabulations	Needell, B., et al. (2001). Performance Indicators for Child Welfare Services in California: First Entries to Foster Care 1988-1999; First Entries, Child Population, and Incidence Rates	Not applicable	Not applicable
	US	Data not available	Not applicable	Not applicable	Not applicable

7 Youth arrests for violent crimes	LA	Published tabulations	California Criminal Justice Profile 1999, Criminal Justice Statistics Center, CA Department of Justice	Not applicable	Not applicable
	CA	Published tabulations	California Criminal Justice Profile 1999. Criminal Justice Statistics Center, CA Department of Justice. http://justice/hdcdojnet.state.ca.us/cjsc_stats/prof99/19/3C.htm. downloaded 7/3/01	Not applicable	Not applicable
	US	Tabulations based on reported national numbers with LA County numbers subtracted out	Not applicable	Adapted from Snyder, H. (2000) Juvenile Arrests, 1999. Washington, DC: Office of Juvenile Justice and Delinquency Prevention. Internet citation: OJJDP Statistical Briefing Book. December 2000. Online at http://ojjdp.ncjrs.org/ojstatbb/html/qa276.html	U.S. Bureau of the Census, U.S. Population Estimates, by Age, Sex, Race, and Hispanic Origin: 1980-1999. [machine-readable data files released April 11, 2000]
8 Homicide rate	LA	Tabulations	Not applicable	Los Angeles County Department of Health Services, Public Health Programs and Services, Health Assessment & Epidemiology, 313 North Figueroa Street, Room 127	Walter R. MacDonald & Associates
	CA	Published tabulations		Not applicable	Not applicable
	US	Published tabulations		Not applicable	Not applicable
9 Adults employed by quarter***	LA	Tabulations based on micro data files	Not applicable	Current Population Survey, March Supplement	Current Population Survey, March Supplement
	CA	Tabulations based on micro data files	Not applicable	Current Population Survey, March Supplement	Current Population Survey, March Supplement
	US	Tabulations based on micro data files	Not applicable	Current Population Survey, March Supplement	Current Population Survey, March Supplement
10 Annual income under poverty level	LA	Tabulations based on micro data files	Not applicable	Current Population Survey, March Supplement	Current Population Survey, March Supplement
	CA	Tabulations based on micro data files	Not applicable	Current Population Survey, March Supplement	Current Population Survey, March Supplement
	US	Tabulations based on micro data files	Not applicable	Current Population Survey, March Supplement	Current Population Survey, March Supplement
11 Percentage of family income used for housing	LA	Tabulations based on micro data files	American Housing Survey	American Housing Survey	Not applicable
	CA	Tabulations based on micro data files	American Housing Survey	American Housing Survey	Not applicable
	US	Tabulations based on micro data files	American Housing Survey	American Housing Survey	Not applicable
12 Personal behavior harmful to self or others: child abuse	LA	Tabulations based on aggregate data	Not applicable	Department of Children and Family Services, Statistics Section, Los Angeles County. Data prepared for California DSS Annual Reprot SOC 291. Preplacement Preventive Services	Race/Ethnic Population with Age and Sex Detail, 1970-2040. State of California, Department of Finance, December 1998. http://www.dof.ca.gov/html/demograp/data.htm
	CA	Published tabulations	US, DHHS, Administration on Children, Youth, and Families, National Child Abuse and Neglect Data System	Not applicable	Not applicable
	US	Published tabulations	US, DHHS, Administration on Children, Youth, and Families, National Child Abuse and Neglect Data System	Not applicable	Not applicable
13 Participation in community activities	LA	Tabulations based on micro data files	Not applicable	Current Population Survey, November Voting and Registration Supplement	Current Population Survey, November Voting and Registration Supplement
	CA	Tabulations based on micro data files	Not applicable	Current Population Survey, November Voting and Registration Supplement	Current Population Survey, November Voting and Registration Supplement
	US	Tabulations based on micro data files	Not applicable	Current Population Survey, November Voting and Registration Supplement	Current Population Survey, November Voting and Registration Supplement

Indicator	Geo				
14 Adult education; attainment of high school diploma, GED, or 8th grade reading level	LA	Tabulations based on micro data files	Not applicable	Current Population Survey, March Supplement	Current Population Survey, March Supplement
	CA	Tabulations based on micro data files	Not applicable	Current Population Survey, March Supplement	Current Population Survey, March Supplement
	US	Tabulations based on micro data files	Not applicable	Current Population Survey, March Supplement	Current Population Survey, March Supplement
15 Elementary and secondary school students reading at grade level	LA	Tabulations based on aggregate data	Not applicable	Standardized Testing and Reporting Program (STAR), California Department of Education, Available online at: http://star.cde.ca.gov	Standardized Testing and Reporting Program (STAR), California Department of Education, Available online at: http://star.cde.ca.gov
	CA	Tabulations based on aggregate data	Not applicable	Standardized Testing and Reporting Program (STAR), California Department of Education, Available online at: http://star.cde.ca.gov	Standardized Testing and Reporting Program (STAR), California Department of Education, Available online at: http://star.cde.ca.gov
	US	Data not available	Not applicable	Not applicable	Not applicable
16 Teenage high school graduation	LA	Tabulations based on aggregate data	Not applicable	Education Demographics Unit, California Department of Education. Available online through Dataquest at http://data1.cde.ca.gov/dataquest/	Education Demographics Unit, California Department of Education. Available online through Dataquest at http://data1.cde.ca.gov/dataquest/
	CA	Tabulations based on aggregate data	Not applicable	Education Demographics Unit, California Department of Education. Available online through Dataquest at http://data1.cde.ca.gov/dataquest/	Education Demographics Unit, California Department of Education. Available online through Dataquest at http://data1.cde.ca.gov/dataquest/
	US	Data not available	Not applicable	Not applicable	Not applicable
17 Mother's educational attainment at child's birth	LA	Tabulations based on micro data files	California Birth Statistical Master File, CA Department of Health Services, Office of Health Information and Research	Not applicable	Not applicable
	CA	Tabulations based on micro data files	California Birth Statistical Master File, CA Department of Health Services, Office of Health Information and Research	Not applicable	Not applicable
	US	Data not available	Not applicable	Not applicable	Not applicable
18 Adult participation in education or vocational training	LA	Tabulations based on micro data files	Not applicable	Current Population Survey, October Education Supplement	Current Population Survey, October Education Supplement
	CA	Tabulations based on micro data files	Not applicable	Current Population Survey, October Education Supplement	Current Population Survey, October Education Supplement
	US	Tabulations based on micro data files	Not applicable	Current Population Survey, October Education Supplement	Current Population Survey, October Education Supplement

*Level of Geography: LA = Los Angeles County, CA = Rest of California, US = Rest of Nation

**Values/rates taken from published sources, not calculated by RAND

***The indicator is measured at the annual level, rather than quarterly

REFERENCES

Abrams, B. and S. Selvin, "Maternal Weight Gain Pattern and Birth Weight," *American Journal of Obstetrics and Gynecology, 86*(2):163–169, 1995.

Alexander, G.R. and C.C. Korenbrot, "The Role of Prenatal Care in Preventing Low Birth Weight," *The Future of Children: Low Birth Weight, 5*(1):103–120, Los Altos, CA: Center for the Future of Children, The David and Lucile Packard Foundation, 1995.

Bachman, R. and A.L. Coker, "Police Involvement in Domestic Violence: The Interactive Effects of Victim Injury, Offender's History of Violence, and Race," *Violence and Victims, 10*: 91–106, 1995.

Black, D. and A. Reiss, "Police Control of Juveniles," *American Sociological Review, 35*: 63–77, 1970.

Blank, R.M., "Why Were Poverty Rates So High in the 1980s?" in Dimitri Papadimitriou and Edward N. Wolff, eds., *Poverty and Prosperity in the USA in the Late Twentieth Century*, New York and London: Macmillan, 1993.

Blank, R.M., "Fighting Poverty: Lessons from Recent U.S. History," *The Journal of Economic Perspectives, 14*(2):3–19, 2000.

Blank, R.M. and A. Blinder, "Macroeconomics, Income Distribution and Poverty," in Sheldon H. Danziger and Daniel H. Weinberg, eds., *Fighting Poverty: What Works and What Doesn't?*, Cambridge, MA: Harvard University Press, 1986.

Brooks, L.W., "Police Discretionary Behavior: A Study of Style," in R.G. Dunham and G.P. Alpert, eds., *Thinking About Police: Contemporary Readings* Prospect Heights, IL: Waveland Press, pp. 149–166, 1997.

Buzawa, E.S., T.L. Austin, and C.G. Buzawa, "Responding to Crimes of Violence against Women: Gender Differences versus Organizational Imperatives," *Crime and Delinquency, 41*: 443–467, 1995.

Canton, D. and J. Lynch, "Self-Report Surveys as Measures of Crime and Criminal Victimization," in D. Duffee, ed., *Measurement and Analysis of Crime and Justice*, pp. 85–138, Washington, D.C.: U.S. Department of Justice, National Institute of Justice, 2000.

Card, David and Alan Krueger, "Labor Market Effects of School Quality: Theory and Evidence," in Gary Burtless, ed., *Does Money Matter? The Effect of*

School Resources on Student Achievement and Adult Success, Washington, DC: Brookings Institution Press, 1996.

Chaffin, M., K. Kelleher, and J. Hollenberg, "Onset of Physical Abuse and Neglect: Psychiatric, Substance Abuse, and Social Risk Factors from Prospective Community Data," *Child Abuse & Neglect, 20*(3):191–203, 1996.

Chomitz, V.R., L.W.Y. Cheung, and E. Lieberman, "The Role of Lifestyle in Preventing Low Birth Weight," *The Future of Children: Low Birth Weight, 5*(1):121–138, Los Altos, CA: Center for the Future of Children, The David and Lucile Packard Foundation, 1995.

Collins, J.W., Jr. and R.J. David, "The Differential Effect of Traditional Risk Factors on Infant Birth Weight among Blacks and Whites in Chicago," *American Journal of Public Health, 80*(6):679, 1990.

Coulton, C.J., J.E. Korbin, and M. Su, "Neighborhoods and Child Maltreatment: A Multi-Level Study," *Child Abuse and Neglect, 23*(11):1019–1040, 1999.

Council of Economic Advisers, *Economic Report of the President, February 1999*, Washington, D.C.: U.S. Government Printing Office, 1999.

Currie, J. and J. Gruber, "Saving Babies: The Efficacy and Cost of Recent Changes in the Medicaid Eligibility of Pregnant Women," *Journal of Political Economy, 104*(6):1263-1296, 1994.

Devaney, B., "Very Low Birth Weight among Medicaid Newborns in Five States," *The Effects of Prenatal WIC Participation*, Vol. 2, Washington, D.C.: U.S. Department of Agriculture, Food and Nutrition Service, 1992.

Dickert, S., S. Houser, and J.K. Scholz, "The Earned Income Tax Credit and Transfer Programs: A Study of Labor Market and Program Participation," *Tax Policy and the Economy, 9*:1–50, 1995.

Dore, M.M., "Family Preservation and Poor Families: When 'Homebuilding' Is Not Enough," *Families in Society, 74*(9):545–556, 1993.

Drake, B. and S. Pandey, "Understanding the Relationship between Neighborhood Poverty and Specific Types of Child Maltreatment," *Child Abuse & Neglect, 20*(11):1003–1018, 1996.

Ebrahim, S.H., E.T. Luman, and R.L. Floyd, "Alcohol Consumption by Pregnant Women in the United States during 1988–1995," *Obstetrics and Gynecology, 92*(2):187–192, 1998.

Eckenrode, J., B. Ganzel, C. Henderson, E. Smith, D. Olds, J. Powers, R. Cole, H. Kitzman, and K. Sidora, "Preventing Child Abuse and Neglect with a

Program of Nurse Home Visitation: The Limiting Effects of Domestic Violence," *JAMA: Journal of the American Medical Association, 284*(11):1385–1391, 2000.

Eide, E.R. and N. Ronan, "Is Participation in High School Athletics an Investment or a Consumption Good? Evidence from High School and Beyond," Forthcoming, *Economics of Education Review*, 2001.

Eide, E.R. and M.H. Showalter, "The Effect of Grade Retention on Educational and Labor Market Outcomes," Forthcoming, *Economics of Education Review*, 2001.

Eissa, N. and H.W. Hoynes, *The Earned Income Tax Credit and the Labor Supply of Married Couples*, Department of Economics, University of California, Berkeley, 1998.

Eissa, N. and J.B. Liebman, "Labor Supply Response to the Earned Income Tax Credit, *Quarterly Journal of Economics, 111*(2):605–637, 1996.

English, D., D. Marshall, and M. Orme, "Characteristics of Repeated Referrals to Child Protective Services in Washington State," *Child Maltreatment, 4*(4):297–307, 1999.

Felson, R.B., S.F. Messner, and A. Hoskin, "The Victim-Offender Relationship and Calling the Police in Assaults," *Criminology, 37*: 931–947, 1999.

Fiscella K., "Does Prenatal Care Improve Birth Outcomes? A Critical Review," *Obstetrics and Gynecology, 85*:468–479, 1995.

Frick, K.D. and P.M. Lantz, "Selection Bias in Prenatal Care Utilization: An Interdisciplinary Framework and Review of the Literature," *Medical Care Research and Review, 53*(4):371–396, 1996.

Friedman, M., *Results and Performance Accountability Implementation Guide*, Fiscal Policy Studies Institute, http://www.raguide.org/, 2001.

Frisch, L.A. and J.M. Caruso, "The Criminalization of Women Battering: Planned Change Experiences in New York State," in A. R. Roberts, ed., *Helping Battered Women: New Perspectives and Remedies*, New York: Oxford University Press, 1992.

Fyfe, J.J., D.A. Klinger, and J.M. Flavin, "Differential Treatment of Male-on-Female Spousal Violence," *Criminology, 35*: 455–473, 1997.

Garbarino, J. and D. Sherman, "High-Risk Neighborhoods and High-Risk Families: The Human Ecology of Child Maltreatment," *Child Development, 51*:188–198, 1980.

Garner, J.H. and C.D. Maxwell, "What Are the Lessons of the Police Arrest Studies?" in S.K. Ward & D. Finkelhor, eds., *Program Evaluation and Family Violence Research*, Binghamton, NY: Haworth Press, 2000.

Garner, J.H., L.J. Hickman, S.S. Simpson, D.J. Woods, and L.C. Allen, "Encouraging Arrest for Domestic Violence in Maryland: An Evaluation," Baltimore, MD: State of Maryland Governor's Office of Crime Control and Prevention, 1999.

Gelles, R.J., "Poverty and Violence toward Children," *American Behavioral Scientist, 35*(3):258–274, 1992.

Gillham, B., G. Tanner, B. Cheyne, I. Freeman, M. Rooney, and A. Lambie, "Unemployment Rates, Single Parent Density, and Indices of Child Poverty: Their Relationship to Different Categories of Child Abuse and Neglect," *Child Abuse & Neglect, 22*(2):79–90, 1998.

Greenfeld, L.A., M.R. Rand, D. Craven, P.A. Klaus, C.A. Perkins, C. Ringel, G. Warchol, C. Maston, and J.A. Fox, *Violence against Intimates: Analysis of Data on Crimes by Current or Former Spouses, Boyfriends, and Girlfriends*, Washington, D.C.: Bureau of Justice Statistics, U.S. Department of Justice, 1998.

Grissom, J.B. and L.A. Shepard, "Repeating and Dropping Out of School," in L.A. Shepard and M.L. Smith, eds., *Flunking Grades: Research and Policies on Retention*, pp. 34–63, London: Falmer, 1989.

Hack, M., N.K. Klein, and H.G. Taylor, "Long-Term Developmental Outcomes of Low Birth Weight," *The Future of Children: Low Birth Weight, 5*(1):176–196, Los Altos, CA: Center for the Future of Children, The David and Lucile Packard Foundation, 1995.

Hanushek, E. (1996), "School Resources and Student Performance," in Gary Burtless, ed., *Does Money Matter? The Effect of School Resources on Student Achievement and Adult Success*, Washington, D.C.: Brookings Institution Press, 1996.

Harris, J.E., "Prenatal Medical Care and Infant Mortality," in V.R. Fuchs, ed., *Economic Aspects of Health*, Chicago, IL: University of Chicago Press, 1982.

Haveman, R. and J. Schwabish, "Macroeconomic Performance and the Poverty Rate: A Return to Normalcy?" Madison, WI: Institute for Research on Poverty, University of Wisconsin, Discussion Paper 1187–1199, 1999.

Healey, K., C. Smith, and C. O'Sullivan, *Batterer Intervention: Program Approaches and Criminal Justice Strategies*, Washington, D.C.: National Institute of Justice, 1998.

Hedderson, John, and Robert F. Schoeni, *LTFSS Plan Countywide Evaluation: Indicators, Data Sources, and Geographical Units of Analysis*, Santa Monica, CA: RAND, DRU-2797-LTFSSP, July 2001.

Herbert, M.K., *Report on Arrests for Domestic Violence in California, 1998*, Criminal Justice Statistics Center, California Department of Justice, 1999.

Hughes, D. and L. Simpson, "The Role of Social Change in Preventing Low Birth Weight," *The Future of Children: Low Birth Weight, 5*(1):87–102, Los Altos, CA: Center for the Future of Children, The David and Lucile Packard Foundation, 1995.

Hutchison, I.W., *Substance Use and Abused Women's Utilization of the Police.* Unpublished paper presented at the American Society of Criminology Conference, Washington, D.C., 1998.

Jewell, S.E. and R. Yip, "Increasing Trends in Plural Births in the United States," *Obstetrics and Gynecology, 85*(2):229–232, 1995.

Johnson, I.M., "A Loglinear Analysis of Abused Wives' Decisions to Call the Police in Domestic Violence Disputes," *Journal of Criminal Justice, 18*:147–159, 1990.

Jones, L. and D. Finkelhor, "The Decline in Child Sexual Abuse Cases," *OJJDP Bulletin*, NCJ 184741, 1–12, January 2001.

Kantor, G.K. and M.A. Straus, "Response of Victims and Police to Assaults on Wives, in M.A. Straus and R.A. Gelles, eds., *Physical Violence In American Families: Risk Factors and Adaptations to Violence in 8,145 Families,* New Brunswick, NJ: Transaction Publishers, pp. 473–487, 1990.

Kaufman, P., J.Y. Kwon, S. Klein, and C.D. Chapman, *Dropout Rates in the United States: 1999*, NCES 2001-022, Washington, D.C.: U.S. Department of Education, National Center for Education Statistics, 2000.

Klinger, D.A., "More on Demeanor and Arrest in Dade County," *Criminology, 34*:61–82, 1996.

Korbin, J. and C. Coulton, *Final Report: Neighborhood and Household Factors in the Etiology of Child Maltreatment*, National Center of Child Abuse and Neglect, Department of Health and Human Services (Grant #90CA1548), 1999.

Kramer, M.S., "Determinants of Low Birth Weight: Methodological Assessment and Meta-Analysis," *Bulletin of the World Health Organization, 5*:663–737, 1987.

Lee, B. and R. Goerge, "Poverty, Early Childbearing and Child Maltreatment: A Multinomial Analysis," *Children & Youth Services Review, 21*(9–10):755–780, 1999.

Lewit, E.M., L.S. Baker, H. Corman, and P.H. Shiono, "The Direct Cost of Low Birth Weight," *The Future of Children: Low Birth Weight, 5*(1):87–102, Los Altos, CA: Center for the Future of Children, The David and Lucile Packard Foundation, 1995.

Los Angeles County Children's Planning Council and United Way of Greater California, *Laying the Groundwork for Change: Los Angeles County's First Action Plan for Its Children, Youth and Families*, 1998.

Los Angeles Department of Public Social Services, http://dpss.co.la.ca.us/urd/chart_six.cfm (accessed 8/6/01).

Lundman, R., R.E. Sykes, and J.P. Clark, "Police Control of Juveniles," *Journal of Research in Crime and Delinquency, 15*:74–91, 1978.

McLaughlin, F.J., W.A. Altemeier, M.J. Christensen, et al., "Randomized Trial of Comprehensive Prenatal Care for Low-Income Women: Effect on Infant Birth Weight," *Pediatrics, 89*(1):128–132, 1992.

Marin, J.A. and M.M. Park, "Trends in Twin and Triplet Births, 1980-1997," *National Vital Statistics Reports, 47*(24), Hyattsville, MD: National Center for Health Statistics, 1999.

Meyer, B. and D.T. Rosenbaum, *Welfare, the Earned Income Tax Credit, and the Employment of Single Mothers*, Evanston, IL: Department of Economics, Northwestern University, 1998.

Mignon, S.I. and W.M. Holmes, "Police Response to Mandatory Arrest Laws," *Crime and Delinquency, 41*(4):430–442, 1995.

Mills, J.L., B.I. Graubard, and E.E. Harley, "Maternal Alcohol Consumption and Birthweight: How Much Drinking During Pregnancy is Safe?," *Journal of the American Medical Association, 252*(14):1875–1879, 1984.

National Center for Education Statistics, Statistical Analysis Report 97-473, July 1997.

National Education Goals Panel, *National Education Goals Report: Building a Nation of Learners, 1999*, Washington, D.C.: U.S. Government Printing Office, 1999.

Needell, B., S. Cuccaro-Alamin, A. Brookhart, and S. Lee, "Transitions from AFCD to Child Welfare in California," *Children and Youth Services Review, 21*(9–10):815–841, 1999.

New Directions Task Force, *Long-Term Family Self-Sufficiency Plan,* County of Los Angeles, October 1999.

Olds, D.L., C.R. Henderson, R. Tatelbaum, and R. Chamberlin, "Improving the Delivery of Prenatal Care and Outcomes of Pregnancy: A Randomized Trial of Nurse Home Visitation," *Pediatrics, 77*(1):16–28, 1986.

Paneth, N.S., "The Problem of Low Birth Weight," *The Future of Children: Low Birth Weight, 5*(1):19–34, Los Altos, CA: Center for the Future of Children, The David and Lucile Packard Foundation, 1995.

Paxson, C. and J. Waldfogel, "Welfare Reforms, Family Resources, and Child Maltreatment," mimeo, Princeton, NJ: Princeton University, 2001.

Reiss, A.J. and J.A. Roth, *Understanding and Preventing Violence.* Washington, D.C.: National Academy of Sciences, 1993.

Rennison, C.M., *Criminal Victimization 2000, Changes 1999-2000 with Trends 1993-2000,* Washington, D.C.: Bureau of Justice Statistics, U.S. Department of Justice, 2001.

Roeleveld, N., E. Vingerhoets, G.A. Zielhuis, and F. Gabreels, "Mental Retardation Associated with Parental Smoking and Alcohol Consumption Before, During, and After Pregnancy," *Preventive Medicine, 21*:110–119, 1992.

Sampson, P.D., F.L. Bookstein, H.M. Barr, and A.P. Steissguth, "Prenatal Alcohol Exposure, Birth Weight, and Measures of Child Size from Birth to 14 Years," *American Journal of Public Health, 84*(9):1421–1428, 1994.

Schlesinger, M. and K. Kronebusch, "The Failure of Prenatal Care Policy for the Poor," *Health Affairs, 4*:91–111, 1990.

Sedlak, A.J. and D.D. Broadhurst, *Executive Summary of the Third National Incidence Study of Child Abuse and Neglect,* National Clearinghouse on Child Abuse and Neglect Information, 1996.

Sherman, L.W., *Policing Domestic Violence: Experiments and Dilemmas,* New York: The Free Press, 1992.

Smith, D.A. and C. Visher, "Street-Level Justice: Situational Determinants of Police Arrest Decisions," *Social Problems, 29*:167–177, 1981.

Smith, D.A. and J. Klein, "Police Control of Interpersonal Disputes," *Social Problems, 31*:468–481, 1984.

Straus, M.A. and R.J. Gelles, *Physical Violence in American Families*. New Brunswick, NJ: Transaction Publishers, 1990.

Straus, M.A., R. Gelles, and S. Steinmetz, *Behind Closed Doors: Violence in the American Family*, Garden City, NY: Doubleday Press, 1980.

Tjaden, P. and N. Thoennes, *Extent, Nature, and Consequences of Intimate Partner Violence*, Washington, D.C.: National Institute of Justice, 2000.

U.S. Bureau of the Census, *Poverty in the United States, 1997*, Current Population Reports, 1998.

U.S. Department of Education, *The Condition of Education*, Washington, D.C.: U.S. Government Printing Office, 2000.

U.S. Department of Health and Human Services, "The Health Benefits of Smoking Cessation," DHHS Publication (CDC) 90-8416, Rockville, MD: Office of Smoking and Health, Department of Health and Human Services, 1990.

U.S. Department of Health and Human Services, *Child Maltreatment*, Administration on Child, Youth and Families, Washington, D.C.: U.S. Government Printing Office, 2001.

Ventura, S.J., J.A. Martin, S.C. Curtin, F. Menacker, and B.E. Hamilton, "Births: Final Data for 1999," *National Vital Statistics Reports, 49*(1), Hyattsville, MD: National Center for Health Statistics, 2001.

Waldfogel, J., *The Future of Child Protection: How to Break the Cycle of Abuse and Neglect*, Cambridge, MA: Harvard University Press, 1998.

Wolock, I., P. Sherman, L. Feldman, and B. Metzger, "Child Abuse and Neglect Referral Patterns: A Longitudinal Study," *Children and Youth Services Review, 23*(1):21–47, 2001.

Zuravin, S., "The Ecology of Child Abuse and Neglect: Review of the Literature and Presentation of Data," *Violence and Victims, 4*:101–120, 1989.